PSHE Education for Key Stage 4

LESLEY de MEZA, STEPHEN De SILVA
& PHILIP ASHTON

The Publishers would like to thank the following for permission to reproduce copyright material:
Photo credits: P5 ©dundanim – Fotolia; p6 ©Andres Rodriguez – Fotolia; p11 top ©bociek666 – Fotolia; p11 bottom ©LifeStyle/Alamy; p12 ©Julián Rovagnati – Fotolia; p13 left Reproduced with kind permission of Keep Britain Tidy; p13 right Reproduced with kind permission of Brook Advisory Centres; p16: Wikimedia Public domain/http://commons.wikimedia.org/wiki/File:Leonardo_da_Vinci-_Vitruvian_Man.JPG; p17 ©marksykes – Fotolia; p22 ©Mayan Mushroom Stones, www.mushroom-stones.com; pp24–5 ©Pinosub – Fotolia; p31 ©Sean Gladwell – Fotolia; p32 Anger ©Stockbyte/Photolibrary Group Ltd; p32 Fear ©Dmytro Konstantynov – Fotolia; p32 Sadness ©Imagestate Media; p32 Enjoyment ©Imagestate Media; p32 Love ©Petro Feketa – Fotolia; p32 Disgust ©Anton Gvozdikov – Fotolia; p32 Shame ©Imagestate Media; p32 Surprise ©fotofac – Fotolia; p35 ©Elena Stepanova – Fotolia; p39 top ©brankatekic – Fotolia; p39 bottom ©Yves Damin – Fotolia; p40 ©Olivier – Fotolia; p41 ©Dave Thompson/PA Archive/Press Association Images; p47 ©Imagestate Media; p48 left ©Bosse Haglund/Alamy; p48 centre ©Peter Titmuss/Alamy; p48 right ©Amy Strycula/Alamy; p49 ©Gilbert 2005/Grief Encounter Project; p50 top ©Elenathewise – Fotolia; p50 centre ©FutureDigitalDesign – Fotolia.com; p50 bottom ©Yuri Arcurs – Fotolia; p51 top ©Photodisc/Getty Images; p51 centre ©Rob – Fotolia; p51 bottom ©Photodisc/Getty Images; p52 left ©Cultura/Alamy; p52 centre left ©Visions of America, LLC/Alamy; p52 centre right Mariusz Blach – Fotolia; p52 right ©Caroline Sylger Jones/Alamy; p53 ©Kablonk Micro – Fotolia; p60 top Reproduced with kind permission of The Survivors Trust; p60 bottom Reproduced with kind permission of Kidscape; p61 top Reproduced with kind permission of the Men's Advice Line; p61 bottom Reproduced with kind permission of Women's Aid; p62 ©zirconicusso – Fotolia; p63 ©CARL DE SOUZA/AFP/Getty Images; p64 ©Boitano Photography/Alamy; p65 ©PA Archive/Press Association Images; p66 Reproduced with kind permission of CHIVA; p67 ©Ferdaus Shamim/WireImage/Getty Images; p71 1 ©claireliz – Fotolia; p71 2 ©S. Mohr Photography – Fotolia; p71 3 ©gunnar3000 – Fotolia; p71 4 ©SunnyS – Fotolia; p71 5 ©Stockbyte/Photolibrary Group Ltd; p71 6 ©Couperfield – Fotolia; p73 ©Bronwyn Photo – Fotolia; p75 top ©JJAVA – Fotolia; p75 bottom ©photomic – Fotolia; p76 ©TheStockCube – Fotolia; p80 ©Monkey Business – Fotolia; p90 right ©Brand X/Corbis; p90 left ©Image Source/Getty Images; p91 top ©Catherine Yeulet/iStockphoto; p91 bottom ©Photodisc/Getty Images; p103 ©David Fisher/Rex Features; p119 top ©KonstantinosKokkinis – Fotolia; p119 centre ©Ivan Kruk – Fotolia; p119 bottom ©Monkey Business – Fotolia.com; p120 ©Tim Rooke/Rex Features; p123 ©iQoncept – Fotolia.
Acknowledgements: P4 Kate Fox, extract, adapted from 'Mirror, Mirror' article from www.sirc.org/publik/mirror.html; p9 Times Educational Supplement, '30 Million to 1', article from www.tes.co.uk/rticle.aspx?storycode=2332899; p15 article about James from http://diana-award.org.uk/award-holders/person-number-one, reproduced by permission of The Diana Award; pp24–5: The drugs economy, based on an activity originally published in DrugWise – 1986 ISDD/SCODA/TACADE, reproduced by permission of DrugScope; p27 'Your problems, your solutions: Is giving 15-year-olds alcohol at a party OK?' from The Guardian, 9 February 2008, copyright Guardian News & Media Ltd 2008, reproduced by permission of GNM; pp28–9: Legislation timeline from Factsheet: Institute of Alcohol Studies, 16 January 2009; p34: Problems making friends from www.bbc.co.uk/radio1/advice/factfile_az/problems_making_friends, reproduced by permission of the BBC; p45 The SUMO principles from www.thesumoguy.com, reproduced by permission; p66 Schools close doors on HIV charity's kids camp from Times Educational Supplement, 21 May 2010; p69 James Berry, 'What Do We Do with a Variation?' from When I Dance (Hamish Hamilton, 1988); p71 Issues scenarios from Beliefs, Values and Attitudes (Me-and-Us Ltd, 2009), reproduced by permission of the publisher; p93 Leaving home at 18, based upon an original article from www.thesite.org, a UK website supporting 16 to 25 year olds. Information was correct at time of going to print and written for a UK audience, reproduced by permission of YouthNet; pp124–5 PFEG definitions from www.pfeg.org, reproduced by kind permission of pfeg (Personal Finance Education Group). Crown copyright material is reproduced under Class Licence Number C02P0000060 with the permission of the Controller of HMSO.

Orders: please contact Bookpoint Ltd, 130 Milton Park, Abingdon, Oxon OX14 4SB. Telephone: (44) 01235 827720. Fax: (44) 01235 400454. Lines are open 9.00–5.00, Monday to Saturday, with a 24-hour message answering service. Visit our website at www.hoddereducation.co.uk

First published in 2011 by
Hodder Education,
An Hachette UK Company
338 Euston Road
London NW1 3BH

Impression number 5 4 3 2 1
Year 2015 2014 2013 2012 2011

Cover photo © ImageZoo Illustration/Veer
Illustrations by Oxford Designers and Illustrators, Richard Duszczak, Barry Glennard, Greengate Publishing Services, Alex Machin, Steve Parkhouse at Daedalus Studios & Stephanie Strickland
Text design and layouts bt Julie Martin
Printed in Italy

A catalogue record for this title is available from the British Library

ISBN: 978 1444 12074 5

Contents

Introduction

Personal, Social, Health and Economic education (PSHE education) is part of our personal development. Personal development happens throughout our lives – in school, when we are with our friends, working, shopping, socialising, etc.

PSHE education is the part of personal development that happens in the school curriculum. There are two Programmes of Study for PSHE education and this book will support you in developing the knowledge, skills and attributes identified in those Programmes of Study. These are:

Personal Well-being – helps young people embrace change, feel positive about themselves and enjoy healthy, safe, responsible and fulfilled lives.

Economic Well-being and Financial Capability – aims to equip young people with the knowledge and skills to make the most of changing opportunities in learning, work and personal finance.

These two Programmes of Study are covered in eleven chapters:

1. The Media and Young People
2. Healthy Choices
3. Emotional and Mental Health
4. Relationships
5. Diversity
6. Values
7. Consumerism
8. Personal Finance
9. The Future
10. Employability
11. Business and Enterprise

Each chapter is divided into a series of topics that include a range of issues for you to consider. The topics are designed to:

- help you focus on the main points you need to learn by providing you with learning objectives and structuring the activities around them
- give you the opportunity to develop the skills you need through a variety of activities
- encourage you to feel confident in sharing your thoughts and feelings in a supportive atmosphere.

The book's active learning opportunities are designed to help you:

- recognise and manage risk
- take increasing personal responsibility in your choices and behaviours
- make positive contributions to your family, school and community
- begin to understand the nature of the world of work, the diversity and function of business and its contribution to national prosperity
- develop as a questioning and informed consumer
- learn to manage your money and finances effectively.

Your teacher may decide to undertake a summative assessment task in some or all of the chapters. These will be linked to the End of Key Stage Statements for PSHE education. This will give you feedback on how you are progressing through the course.

PSHE education deals with real-life issues that affect all of us, our families and our communities. It engages with the social and economic realities of our lives, experiences and attitudes. Could there be a more important subject to study?

1 The Media and Young People

Body image

In this topic you will learn about:

- how the media influences the way we see ourselves
- how issues of 'body image' in the media affect people's health.

You will explore:

- whether males and females feel differently about body image
- how the 'deficit model' is used to sell things to us.

Source 1

Media: Communication channels through which news, entertainment, education, data or promotional messages are disseminated. Media includes every broadcasting medium such as newspapers, magazines, TV, music video, radio, billboards, direct mail, telephone, fax and internet.

Body image: The picture each of us has in our head of how we look – our appearance, our shape, our size – and how we feel and think about our body.

What is 'body image'?

1. **a)** Do you agree with the definition of body image in Source 1? Why/Why not?
   b) Come up with an alternative and perhaps better definition of body image.
2. Do you think young people generally have a positive or negative body image? Give two examples to explain your answer.
3. What part do you think the media plays in forming our body image?

Throughout history there have been changing fashions in clothes and in what people perceive as the perfect body shape. In modern times the media has had an increasingly strong influence on our ideas of the perfect body and what we should look like. It often presents different **celebrities** as conforming, or not, to this 'perfect' image, which is not necessarily healthy to achieve:

The body fat of models and actresses portrayed in the media is at least 10 per cent less than that of healthy women.

(British Medical Association, 2000)

ACTIVITY

What is normal?

4. In groups:

a) Choose one of the following different categories of celebrity:

- Actors/Actresses
- Sportsmen/Sportswomen
- TV personalities
- Musicians/Popstars

b) Brainstorm the names of as many people as you can think of who fit into your category.

c) Organise the names of your celebrities under the most appropriate heading below.

Underweight	Normal	Overweight

d) Discuss the following:

- If a column has more names than all the others, why do you think this is?
- Can you name any other celebrities to fit into columns where few names appear?
- Are there any 'normal' celebrities?

You may have found that the results of the last activity point to a uniformity in the way most celebrities look and are presented in the media. Although there are exceptions, this results in an overall image of slim people being the attractive norm (see Source 2).

Source 2

Why all the fuss about body image?

Human beings have always been concerned about appearance – the majority of people want to appear attractive to themselves and others. The problem now is the *degree* of concern. Advances in technology and in particular the rise of the mass media have caused normal concerns about how we look to become obsessions. For example:

- Thanks to the media, we have become accustomed to extremely rigid and uniform standards of beauty.
- TV, billboards, magazines, etc. mean that we see 'beautiful people' all the time – more often than members of our own family – making exceptional good-looks seem real, normal and attainable.
- Standards of beauty have in fact become harder and harder to attain, particularly for women. The current media ideal of thinness for women is achievable by less than five percent of the female population.

Made-up to perfection – the artist's brush, clever lighting and post-production air-brushing can all create the illusion of perfection

Adapted from 'Mirror, Mirror', an article by Kate Fox published by the Social Issues Research Centre, Oxford (www.sirc.org/publik/mirror.html)

ACTIVITY

Media influence

5. a) Read Source 2. Do you agree with it? Choose three different types of media from the definition in Source 1 and find two examples from each – one to support and one to disprove the findings of the article.

b) Which examples were easier to find? What does this tell you about media influence on body image?

Source 3

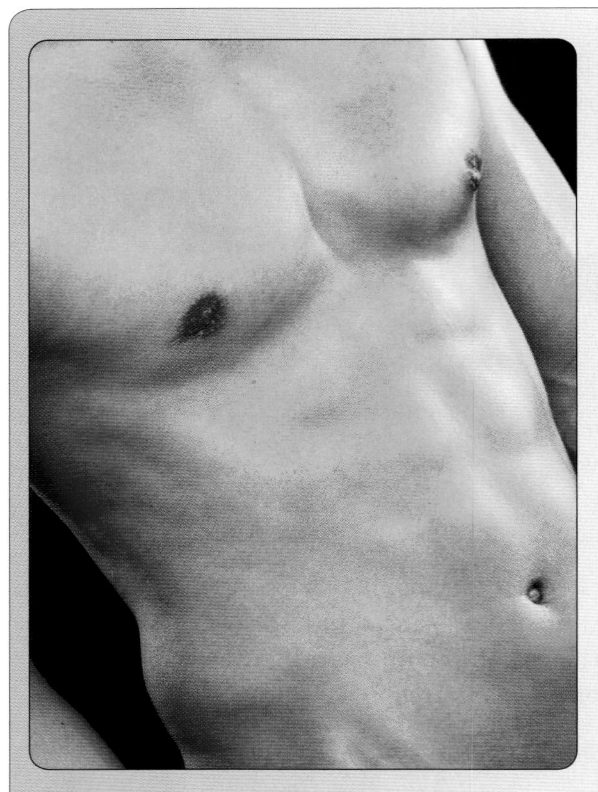

Images such as this could cause body image problems for some men

Body image problems hit men too

People often think it's women rather than men who are most unhappy with their body image. However, all the research says that men are just as likely to be unhappy with the way they look.

In the *British Medical Journal*, experts estimate that three times the number of men suffer from severe dissatisfaction with the way they look compared to 25 years ago. Up to 1 per cent of the male population is estimated to suffer from the disorder in the UK.

Some people think worrying about appearance can seem trivial, but many people who are unhappy about their looks become reluctant to go out – or even attempt suicide. Sufferers can become socially isolated.

Males report being most worried about their skin (because of acne or scarring), going bald, the size or shape of their nose, or their genitals.

The trend for men to look muscular has also caused worries about body image. Some men are becoming preoccupied with their appearance and are spending excessive amounts of time examining, fixing or hiding the perceived defect. Obsessively checking how they look in the mirror, comparing themselves with others and excessive grooming all feed the problem – many men now seek reassurance about how they look.

Is the media creating a '**deficit model**' that we are being sold? That is, we will never be attractive enough? There will always be better soaps to improve our skin; hair products to make us look more attractive; and must-have clothing trends that will instantly make us popular. Source 4 looks at the deficit model and the diet industry.

Can we ever be attractive enough?

6. Read Source 3. In what ways do you think the media has had an influence on how men want to look?
7. Do you think the media target men and women equally? Give reasons for your answers.
8. Read Source 4. How does the diet industry contribute to creating a 'deficit model'?

Source 4

The deficit model and the diet industry

The diet industry in books, fitness videos and specially prepared meals is often our inspiration to get ourselves into shape. But have individuals ever wondered about how the industry is actually contributing to the ever-growing obesity epidemic?

Diets have become like fashion nowadays. New diets seem to pop up every few months; they have even become seasonal. People often talk about this summer's hottest diet or the autumn's secret celebrity diet.

The diet industry knows that only lifestyle changes can permanently let people live healthier lifestyles. But because we are told we only need a few weeks to reach our goal we never really adopt changes that last long.

The diet industry as a whole is a money-spinning industry that has been growing as fast as our country's waist line. The fact is the industry is selling dreams and not solutions for the obesity epidemic. Research suggests 95 per cent of slimmers regain the weight – so does the diet industry rely on failure to make its profits?

Change can only really happen when you take matters into your own hands. Empower yourself to become solely responsible for your health!

ACTIVITY

Happy with who you are

9. How can people learn to be happy with themselves without worrying whether they conform to a certain look or not?

The cult of celebrity

In this topic you will learn about:

- the effect of 'celebrity' on young people's career choices
- the role the media plays in promoting celebrity lifestyles.

You will explore:

- whether young people are overly influenced by glamour and the cult of celebrity
- the connection between actions and consequences when seeking fame.

A survey of 3000 British parents in 2009 commissioned by the TV show *Tarrant Lets the Kids Loose* revealed that many pre-teens had a strong desire to become rich and famous rather than follow more traditional careers. It asked parents what their career hopes and ambitions were when they were young, compared to what their children aspired to. The results are shown in Source 1.

As long ago as February 1968 the artist Andy Warhol said 'In the future everybody will be world famous for fifteen minutes.' Since that time there has been the birth and growth of reality television – this has made fame seem more possible for the general population.

In addition the '**cult of celebrity**' has grown and now reporting on 'celebrities' has become prolific. Young people are encouraged to believe that anyone can become a celebrity – they can become famous for being famous, not necessarily based on talent and ability.

Source 1

Top ten ambitions for young people in 2009 were:

1. **Sportsman 12%**
2. **Pop star 11%**
3. **Actor 11%**
4. **Astronaut 9%**
5. **Lawyer 9%**
6. **Emergency services 7%**
7. **Medicine 6%**
8. **Chef 5%**
9. **Teacher 4%**
10. **Vet 3%**

Top ten ambitions of 25+ years ago were:

1. **Teacher 15%**
2. **Banking/finance 9%**
3. **Medicine 7%**
4. **Scientist 6%**
5. **Vet 6%**
6. **Lawyer 6%**
7. **Sportsman 5%**
8. **Astronaut 4%**
9. **Beautician/hairdresser 4%**
10. **Archaeologist 3%**

ACTIVITY

Career or fame?

1. Look at Source 1.
   a) How have the ambitions for future careers changed over 25 years?
   b) Why do you think they have changed?

Source 2

30 MILLION TO 1

Writing an article about celebrity status, Hannah Frankel suggests that it may be the modern-day addiction but it's schools, not clinics, that often have to pick up the pieces.

It is a phenomenon that is mirrored across the UK. More than one in ten young people would drop education to give fame a shot, according to a Learning and Skills Council survey. Even though the odds of being picked for a reality show and going on to further fame are 30 million to one – worse odds than winning the lottery – about 16 per cent of teenagers believe they will be 'the one'.

Most of the 16 to 19-year-old respondents cited money and success as their main motivating factors, but many hanker after greater recognition and acceptance. More than a quarter of the 777 young people who responded said they saw fame as a way of 'proving other people wrong'; while 19 per cent said it would 'let everyone know who they were'. Roughly 9 per cent said fame would 'help them to feel accepted', and 7 per cent said it would 'make them appear more attractive'.

Nick Williams, the principal of the BRIT school in Croydon, a free performing arts college, says that young people are more astute than we give them credit for. 'Most young people understand the difference between the fantasy life and reality,' he says. 'Celebrity only becomes a corrosive aspect when vulnerable people misunderstand the game.'

Nick insists that most pupils would rather build sustainable careers in the performing arts than become household names. 'We constantly stress that long-term success can only result from genuine talent and incredible hard work,' he argues. 'Only the most tenacious and robust will get there and stay there.'

www.tes.co.uk

ACTIVITY

Reality show or reality life?

2. Read the article in Source 2. Work in small groups to discuss the article and whether you think young people are losing the ability to differentiate between fantasy and reality. Which of the points of view do you agree with – Hannah Frankel or Nick Williams? Give reasons.

Source 3

What do you want to be when you grow up?

In 2007 a primary school teacher in South London discovered the children at her school weren't so interested in career but in lifestyle. The teacher said that 'most wanted to be celebrities and saw physical attractiveness as the key to becoming famous. Few actually considered any skills or talents they would like. It's incredible that children at such a young age had such a want for money and possessions'.

When asked the question 'What do you want to be when you grow up?' answers included the following:

She added 'The majority of the children I spoke to said they wanted to be rich and famous when they grew up. I think the main reason for this is that children lack good role models, in the media especially.'

www.sofeminine.co.uk

Media as role model

3. Read Source 3. Where do young people get their inspiration for future careers?
4. If the media had an obligation to balance its focus on celebrity with positive, everyday, career role models – what would these be?

Source 4

Posed by model

Case study: Mike MacCraigie

Mike MacCraigie is a bright student at a City Academy in the Midlands. Tests predict he should do well in his GCSEs but he struggles to concentrate. Instead, Mike has his eye on becoming a footballer, ideally for his beloved Birmingham City FC.

'Footballers get loads of money and I enjoy playing it as well,' he says. 'Everyone knows who you are when you are a footballer, you are worldwide. I would just love the lifestyle.'

Mike recognises it is tough to make it in football, especially as he does not have a clear idea how to turn professional. He has also been told to have a back-up plan in case his dream does not come true, so he is spending one day a week at Birmingham Metropolitan College, learning about bricklaying and other trades.

The 15-year-old admits he does not always value qualifications. He says: 'You do not need them to become a footballer. All you need is skill.'

ACTIVITY

Pot of gold or own goal?

5. Read Source 4. Mike is thinking of leaving school without taking his GCSEs. What arguments would you use to convince him to think again?

The internet

In the past some celebrities have achieved worldwide fame via the internet. Some careers have taken off as a result – others have crashed. Using the internet can be a double-edged sword. On Facebook and other **social networking** sites photographs of individuals are displayed – sometimes in compromising situations. Recently more and more employers are looking up prospective candidates for jobs before they call them for interview.

Source 5

faceblog

Sarah's great night out!

ACTIVITY

The internet – famous or infamous forever

6. Read the information about the internet and look at Source 5. Even knowing the pitfalls of the internet, why do some people still seek instant fame and celebrity via the web?

Health

In this topic you will learn about:

- the media's role in promoting positive health
- how social marketing is used in health campaigns.

You will explore:

- techniques used in the social marketing of health
- how health campaigns might be made more positive.

The media

The media can play a valuable role in bringing important issues to our attention. This is particularly the case when it comes to health, where the media are used by the government to make people aware of health issues and to try and influence behaviour.

Social marketing

The way that governments have communicated messages about public health changed during the twentieth century from using simple 'finger-wagging' slogans such as 'Don't litter' and 'Stop smoking' to using **social marketing** techniques to persuade people to change their behaviour and engage them with the message.

Social marketing is where adverts and marketing messages are designed to influence behaviours – not to benefit the advertiser, but to benefit the person being targeted by the campaign and society in general. Social marketing campaigns can be taken up by businesses too (see Source 1).

Source 1

The '5 A DAY' healthy eating campaign

Since 2003, The '5 A DAY' programme has aimed to increase awareness of the health benefits of fruit and vegetables and encourage people to eat more of them (at least five portions a day). In particular, the programme has provided clear and consistent messages about portion sizes of fruit and vegetables and what counts towards '5 A DAY'. It has used a variety of media to convey its message:

2003
Posters, postcards, leaflets and brochures were produced.

2004
All 4–6-year-old children in LEA-maintained infant, primary and special schools were entitled to a free piece of fruit or vegetable each school day.

2006
TV adverts such as 'Natural History at the Supermarket' were used, as well as printed materials, targeted at families with children.

2007
Major supermarkets started offering deals to support '5 A DAY' and food manufacturers widely used it as a promotional tool, making statements on their packaging such as 'counts towards 2 of your 5 a day'.

2010
The '5 A DAY' message was very widely recognised by children and adults alike.

Media health campaigns

1. Look at Source 1. Why do you think the '5 A DAY' campaign was so successful in raising awareness about the need to eat more fruit and vegetables?
2. What other government campaigns can you think of that have been targeted at improving people's health/safety? The photos in Source 2 might help you or you could visit the following website, which gives more examples: www.dh.gov.uk/en/MediaCentre/Currentcampaigns/index.htm.
3. Are there any that are targeted particularly at young people? If so, how?
4. Imagine that the government makes a decision that there will only be ONE public health campaign per year aimed at young people of your age. What health message should that campaign convey in the twelve months starting today?

Source 2 Two examples of social marketing

A

B

Language

Another important consideration when devising a health campaign is the language that is used. It could be used to shock, such as 'Dying to take the call?' (an advert against using a mobile phone while driving), or words can be chosen carefully to promote positive responses rather than negative ones. The Liverpool Schools Parliament put forward the idea to the local council of banning the word 'obesity' in their health campaigns and using the term 'unhealthy weight' instead. This is because they think the word 'obesity' puts young people off confronting their weight problems.

ACTIVITY

Analysing social marketing and health

5. Using the images in Source 2 and the information in Source 3, answer the following questions for each image:

a) What is the health issue?

b) What is the message?

c) What technique(s) are being used?

d) How effective do you think this example is in getting people to change their behaviour?

Source 3

Some social marketing techniques

- ✓ Celebrity endorsement – a well-known person says or shows how good something is
- ✓ Voice of authority/scientific evidence – experts (e.g. doctors/scientists) use facts, statistics and research evidence to convince the target audience
- ✓ Band-wagon appeal – implies that because everyone is doing it then you should too
- ✓ Romance/sex appeal – very attractive people and situations are used to gain your attention and influence you
- ✓ Popularity appeal – suggests that if you engage with this you will become more popular
- ✓ Humour – making someone laugh is an effective way of engaging them and makes the issue more memorable/acceptable
- ✓ Distaste – startling, unusual or unpleasant image to gain your attention

ACTIVITY

Using positive language

6. Using the example of the Pig Boy campaign from Source 2 (or one of the campaigns you researched for Activity 2), how could you make the campaign positive rather than negative?

7. Outline a health/safety campaign using a positive approach.

- Decide what health topic you want to draw attention to.
- Decide on the age group you are aiming to reach.
- Decide what important information/message you need to put across.
- Decide the positive features of your campaign and why you think they will work better than a negative approach.

Reporting on young people

In this topic you will learn about:

- how the media portrays young people
- positive media stories about young people.

You will explore:

- positive skills and qualities of yourself and others.

In 2008 a group of young people, funded by the National Youth Agency, published a report on how young people felt they were portrayed in the British media and how this affected their lives. They found that most of the stories about young people were negative; most commonly, stories were about crime, education, gangs or social exclusion, and young offenders in particular were likely to be the subject of negative media portrayal. Source 1 shows what the 700 young people surveyed felt about how they were represented in the media.

Source 1

- 98 per cent of the young people surveyed felt that the media always, often or sometimes represents them as antisocial.
- More than four out of five thought that the media represents them as a group to be feared.
- They felt this may cause older people to be afraid of them and may alienate young people, causing more antisocial behaviour.
- Instead they wanted their achievements to be recognised, and to be given positive attention.
- They also thought that the media represented the majority of them on the behaviour of the minority.

Media Portrayal of Young People – impact and influences, NCB, 2008

The whole picture

1. Read Source 1 above. Discuss each bullet point with a partner – do you agree with the points made? Why/why not?
2. As part of the research into the media and young people, the researchers looked at stories about young people in newspapers over the course of a week and classified them. They found that in one week in 2007, 23 per cent of the stories were positive, 29 per cent were neutral or balanced and 48 per cent were negative.

   In groups, each look at one newspaper every day of a week and cut out the stories on young people. Then classify them into positive, neutral/balanced or negative. Do your findings mirror those in 2007, or is the situation different now?

The media are not always negative about young people. They do tell positive stories as well. Source 2 gives an example.

Source 2

James's story

We never stop being amazed by the power some young people have to push through vital change. That's why we were delighted to give a Diana Award to James, who as a Year 11 student worked with eight others to transform the prefect system in his school.

Up until that point, prefects were seen as a group of older students whose job was to tell other people off. James and his peers decided that wasn't good enough and transformed the system into something to be proud of.

Within a very short time, the younger pupils felt much more safe and secure, knowing that at any lunchtime, break or social event, there would always be a prefect around who could help, give advice or just say 'Hi'. In fact, the new prefects were so popular that they were continually being asked how to apply for the job!

As well as being a prefect, James was also a CHIPS (Childline in Partnership with Schools) counsellor, able to give support to students when they needed a friendly ear, and served for two years on the Billericay Youth Town Council. In the latter role, he helped to organise charity events and worked to improve the facilities around the town for young people.

The Diana Award has been a springboard for James. Through it he has attended a presentation skills training day, attended the national launch of the Award as an independent charity, met minister Ed Miliband, joined the Award's Youth Advisory Board, had lunch with Princes William and Harry, and met many other Award holders.

James can't praise the Award more highly: 'This Award is just fantastic! It really identifies and shows young people all the things they do for others really are appreciated. No matter how big or small the thing that you do, it can still inspire the lives of others. I really hope the Award will grow to become recognised within the UK as the premier award for young people.'

http://diana-award.org.uk/award-holders/person-number-one

Positive people

3. a) Read Source 2 and make a list of all the positive skills and qualities you can find about Tom Gallagher.

b) Which of the qualities and skills do you recognise in yourself? What other positive skills and qualities would you add if the story had been written about you?

4. To counter-balance negative reports about young people, prepare an article for the local media on a positive impact a particular young person, a school or a community group has made in your area.

2 Healthy Choices

Taking responsibility for your health

In this topic you will learn about:

- factors that contribute to a healthy lifestyle.

You will explore:

- individual priorities for keeping healthy
- a self-assessment on healthy eating
- realistic approaches to a healthy future.

Source 1 Health is a whole-person issue

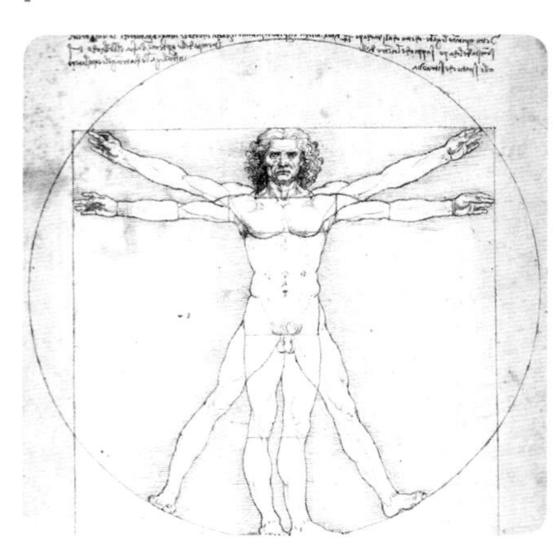

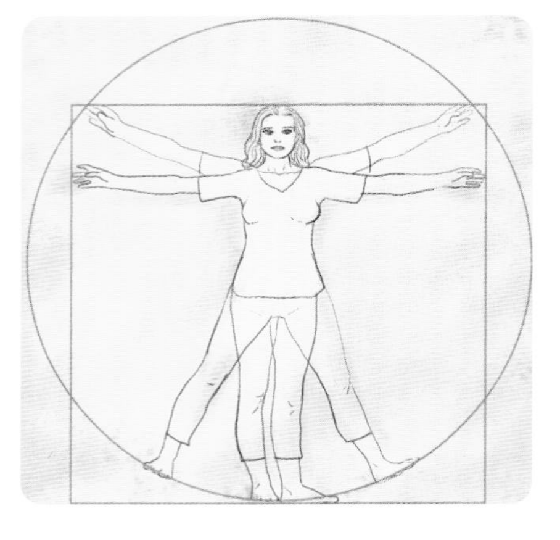

ACTIVITY

What is 'healthy'?

1. Name three things you do that make you healthy and keep you healthy. Categorise them under 'body', 'mind' and 'spirit'.

Look at Source 1. The original Leonardo drawing is commonly used to represent a holistic view of health. By 'holistic' we mean that it is important that health includes more that just the physical body – it is also about the mind and the spirit. It is our mental health and the emotions we experience, along with the physical body, which make up the whole person.

There are many things that contribute to making us healthy and keeping us healthy. Some examples are listed in Source 2.

Source 2 Parts of a healthy lifestyle

a) 5-a-day fruit and vegetables	b) Walking instead of driving/ using the bus	c) A good night's sleep
d) Using the stairs instead of the lift	e) Being able to talk about loss and death	f) Not bottling things up
g) Laughing when you can	h) Access to local healthcare	i) Having interests, hobbies and pastimes
j) A balanced approach to eating	k) Being alcohol aware – and drinking in moderation	l) 30 active minutes five times a week, e.g. swimming, rollerblading, active play, etc.
m) Relaxation – time to chill	n) Going smoke free	o) Feeling loved and loving others

ACTIVITY

Valuing your health

2. Look at Source 2. Which of the three categories of mind, body and spirit would you place each of these under? Can some of them be placed in more than one category?
3. Draw a health pyramid as shown. Put the different ways to good health listed in Source 2 into your health pyramid – making a decision on where each should go. Note that you have 15 ideas but only 10 spaces on your pyramid. Think carefully about which you will choose. Be ready to explain your choices.

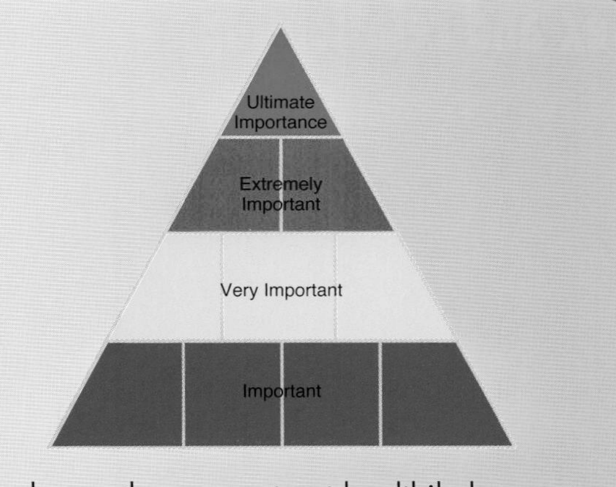

Health pyramid

4. Sometimes people say they cannot eat healthily because fresh and healthy food is more expensive and they don't have the time to cook it from scratch. So what is 'eating healthily' about? Use www.nhs.uk/Tools/Pages/HealthyEating.aspx to find out if you know what eating healthily means. Find out whether you're a healthy eater or could improve your eating patterns.

As a teenager, you are not just growing physically but you are also developing mentally – both your physical brain and your emotions/thought processes (see Source 3). Developing a healthy pattern to your lifestyle now will help you maximise your future potential.

ACTIVITY

Do it now!

5. By now you'll appreciate that you are going through a stage in your life that will affect your future. This is especially true now while your intellectual and physical skills are still developing (see Source 3).

   What healthy habits can a teenager realistically develop now to help them optimise their future health?

Source 3

How's your brain doing?

As a teenager you will probably have heard the expression, 'Grow up and act your age' – well, guess what? ... You probably are doing just that; teenage brains are still under construction!

Previously it was thought that the human brain was fully developed by the time we reach adolescence. We now know this isn't the case. Your brain will not be completely developed until you reach the age of 25. Right now – as an 'adolescent' – is the most important time for your brain development to take place.

Ken Winters, PhD, Mentor Foundation, Department of Psychiatry, University of Minnesota, 2008

Sex and relationships

In this topic you will learn about:

- the age of consent
- contraception
- sexually transmitted infections (STIs).

You will explore:

- the need to think about relationships
- factors that contribute to 'safer sex'
- the choices faced by young people when they have an unplanned pregnancy.

ACTIVITY

Sex – why all the fuss?

1. Based on media reports, soap operas, music videos, etc. what do you think is the average age that young people in the UK have sexual intercourse for the first time? Is it:

- 14.5?
- 15.5?
- 16.5?

(Answer below)

The age of consent

Whoever you are the law says you have to be at least 16 to have sexual intercourse.

People involved in having sex need to give their consent. This means they have freely chosen to be involved. If someone says 'No', it means no! Having sex with somebody who is unable to give their consent is against the law. This might include:

- someone who has a disability or, for whatever reason, is unable to express their wishes
- someone who is 'out of it' for any reason (e.g. alcohol, drugs, etc.). They cannot consent to having sex – so that would be breaking the law too.

Young people aged 16 have reached the 'age of consent'. However, at 16 many students have reported that they have not received much in the way of sex education and have characterised the education they have received in the past as too little, too late and too biological. Some young people say that it would have been good preparation for the future to have been given good, relevant, non-judgemental sex and relationships education.

A 2007 survey of 21,602 young people about sex and relationship education had some of the following feedback:

- 61% of boys and 70% of girls reported not having received any information about personal relationships at school
- 43% of all young people surveyed stated that they hadn't been taught about personal relationships at school
- Max Sztyber (aged 17): 'The education about sex I received was good. I can't really imagine how it could have been much better ... It might have been useful to have more info on STIs though, and we didn't receive anything about relationships.'

UK Youth Parliament Survey: SRE Are You Getting It? (2007)

16.5

Learning about sex and relationships is preparation for the future – it doesn't mean you have to have either now. Each person needs to make a personal decision about when they feel ready. Sex can be a pleasurable experience and there's nothing wrong with waiting until you're older to enjoy it.

> **ACTIVITY**
>
> **Right person; right time; right place; right reason**
>
> **2.** Choose the three statements you most agree with in Source 1 and explain why you agree with them.

Source 1 Talking about relationships and sex

Sexual heath

A **sexually healthy** adult is a person who understands that sex can have various outcomes, ranging from pleasure to conception to transmission of **sexually transmitted infections** (STIs).

The sexually healthy adult engages in:

- active learning
- decision-making
- communication
- behaviours

... that eliminate or reduce the risk of unplanned pregnancy and/or STI transmission.

This is based on the statement of values of the Sexuality Information and Education Council of the US (SIECUS)

> **ACTIVITY**
>
> **How do you keep sexually healthy?**
>
> **3.** Read the statement of values on the left and answer the following questions.
> To keep themselves safe what:
> **a)** does a young person need to know about sex?
> **b)** does a young person need to know about relationships?
> **c)** skills does a young person need?
> **d)** sources of help does a young person need to know about?

Knowing and understanding different contraceptive methods is a basic part of being a sexually healthy adult. Source 2 lists a range of reliable methods of contraception.

Source 2

CONTRACEPTION

Condoms

Condoms are number one for protection against STIs and 98 per cent effective in preventing pregnancy if used correctly every time you have sex.

A condom is made of very thin latex (rubber) or polyurethane. It fits over the man's erect penis. It catches sperm when a man ejaculates and stops it entering his partner. Some condoms are lubricated to make them easier to use.

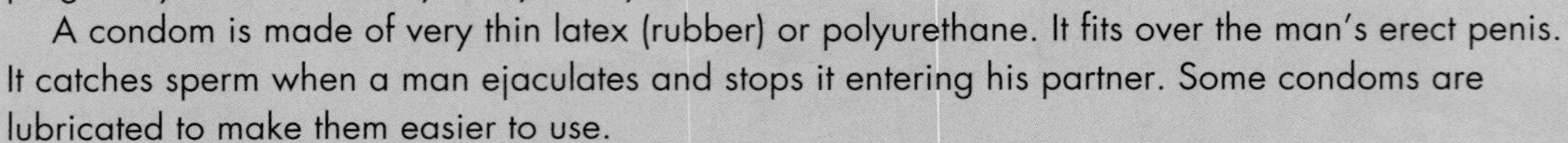

The 'pill'

This is a widely used method of contraception, which is swallowed. It is reliable if it is taken regularly by the person for whom it was prescribed. If that person experiences vomiting or diarrhoea or is prescribed antibiotics, the 'pill' may become ineffective and a doctor should be consulted and another method of contraception used.

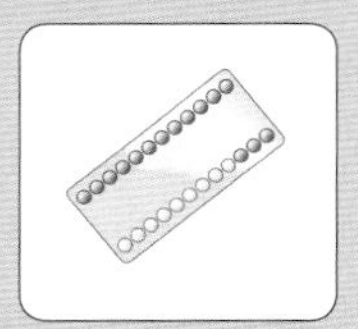

Contraceptive injection

This is an injection given by a nurse or doctor. It is usually renewed every 8–12 weeks and the clinic reminds you when your next injection is due.

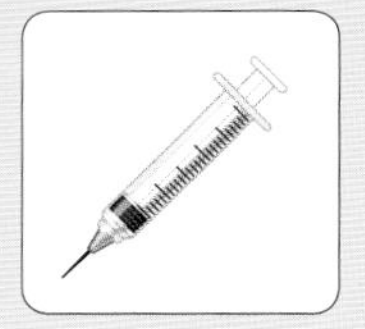

IUS

The Intra Uterine System (IUS) is a small 'T' shaped plastic device containing a hormone. In the past only women who already had children used it – but nowadays it is more widely used for young people. It should only be placed into the womb by a doctor. This is a simple procedure. Once in place it is immediately effective as a method of contraception. It can remain in place for up to five years.

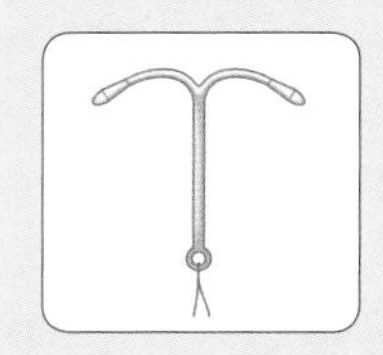

Implant

This is a tiny stick containing a hormone. It is easily placed just under the skin by a nurse or doctor. Once in place it does not need to be renewed for at least 3–5 years.

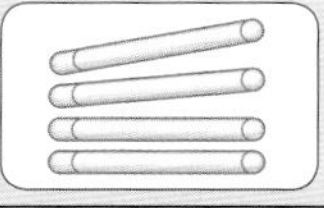

Emergency contraception pill

This should not be used as a routine method of contraception but can provide a back-up if your usual method of contraception has gone wrong. It comprises a pill to be swallowed, which can be taken up to three days after intercourse. It is widely available from GPs, family planning/sexual health clinics, pharmacies and from the A&E department of some hospitals.

Even though people know and understand the range of things that may keep them sexually healthy, sometimes things don't go according to plan and problems occur. Two of the unintended consequences of unsafe sex are sexually transmitted infections (STIs) and unplanned pregnancy.

STIs – Did you know ...

- 70 per cent of women and 50 per cent of men who have an STI may not have any symptoms.
- Chlamydia is now the most common (yet easily curable) STI in the UK and in the last decade the number of people infected with Chlamydia has increased by 206 per cent.
- As many as one in ten young people under 25 may have Chlamydia but don't know it. There aren't always symptoms but an infection could leave you unable to have children.
- There are an estimated 20,000 HIV-positive people in the UK who don't know they've got HIV. It weakens the immune system so that your body finds it harder to fight off other infections. There is no cure.
- You don't need to have lots of sexual partners to get an STI – anyone who has sex without a condom is at risk.

If you have unprotected sex ... think about the following:

- Get yourself checked out – whether you have symptoms or not. Unprotected sex leaves you open to infections.
- If you have itches, sores or blisters around your genitals, you may have an STI. No need to panic, but you do need to contact your local sexual health (GUM) clinic – don't wait to see if it clears up.
- Sexual health check-ups and contraception – including condoms – are free and available to everyone in the UK.
- You can arrange a visit to a sexual health (GUM) clinic any time. It is completely confidential.
- Always use a condom every time you have sex – this is the best way of making sure you don't get a STI.
- Condoms are not just a bloke thing; women buy four out of every ten condoms sold in shops.
- Condoms come in a wide range of sizes, flavours, colours and shapes and are available for both men and women. There are allergy-free versions and even vegan varieties!

ACTIVITY

Unplanned pregnancy

4. Vikki and Joe are looking forward to October – one of them has a place at art college and the other at university. They don't live far apart and their families know each other well. Vikki and Joe have been together since Year 11 and six months ago their relationship became a sexual one. They thought they had their contraception sorted out. So, when Vikki missed a period she didn't panic. But when she missed the next one they were both shocked to find that she was pregnant.

In common with many other young couples in this situation they faced the following options:

- abortion
- adoption
- grandparents bring up baby
- care for the baby themselves.

Consider each option and decide:

a) What might they feel about this?
b) What do they need to think about?
c) What should they do?

Drugs

In this topic you will learn about:

- drugs and the law
- an example of a 'drugs' supply chain'.

You will explore:

- what is meant by a 'drug-taking society'
- drugs and risk.

From ancient times to the present day, people have used drugs for all sorts of purposes. Drugs have always been around – particularly to help cure illnesses and avoid pain, and also for pleasure.

Mushroom stones crafted in Guatemala in 1000 BCE are believed by many to represent psychoactive mushrooms (though these are not original Mayan stones).

ACTIVITY

A drug-using society?

1. It has been said that we live in a drug-using society. Leaving out illegal drugs, discuss whether you think this is true. Use the following ideas to help your discussion:
   - complementary therapies (e.g. plants such as echinacea and arnica) draw on natural remedies to prevent or treat illnesses
   - alcohol and tobacco are widely used recreationally by large numbers of people – people can become dependent on them
   - using over-the-counter medicines (bought from pharmacies, supermarkets, etc.) is a standard way of dealing with feeling unwell
   - walk-in centres and GP practices can supply prescription medicines to treat a wide range of problems – some people become over-reliant and may develop dependency.
2. Have we created a 'pill-for-every-ill' culture?

In our society we do seem to be using **legal drugs** quite regularly. **Illegal drugs** are also prevalent and can cause emotional and physical health problems and sometimes have a negative impact on society. Whether legal or illegal, there is no drug that is risk free.

Drugs risks – true or false?

3. Decide if the following statements are true or false. (Answers below.)

- **a)** Possessing magic mushrooms is not against the law.
- **b)** LSD is not addictive.
- **c)** One of the main dangers of cannabis is the state of intoxication it produces.
- **d)** Injecting can be one of the most dangerous ways of taking drugs.
- **e)** Solvent sniffing is not illegal.
- **f)** It is illegal for a 16-year-old to smoke cigarettes.
- **g)** If a teacher knows a pupil has used illegal drugs they have to tell the police.
- **h)** The police can enter a school and make a search without a warrant.
- **i)** If a pupil tells a teacher that they have used illegal drugs the teacher is legally bound to tell their parents.
- **j)** If a person buys one ecstasy tablet for a friend with the friend's money – that person could be charged with supplying drugs.

Source 1 What's the risk?

1. **Hitesh** is growing cannabis plants in his greenhouse. He probably won't bother to harvest them.

2. **Nancy**'s parents are really 'laid back' about cannabis. They used to smoke it themselves but don't anymore. They don't mind Nancy smoking cannabis in their house – on her own and/or along with her friends.

3. **Jermaine** is into athletics in a big way and takes steroids to improve his performance. He also gets steroids for **Chantal** but doesn't make any profit out of selling them to her.

4. **Lee** bought what he thought was ecstasy from a dealer at a club. In fact it is ketamine.

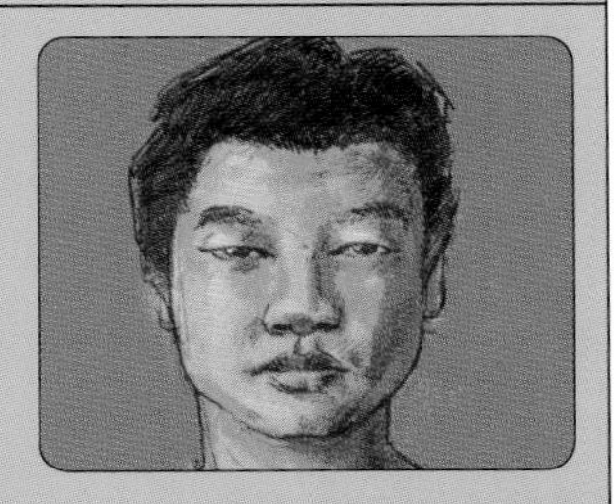

5. **Tony** and **Lorraine** are 17. They go into their local pub and order a pint of beer and a pint of lager at the bar. A police officer walks in.

6. **Damian** is 14 and regularly buys poppers (nitrite) from a local shop.

ACTIVITY

What's the risk?

4. Look at Source 1 and answer the following questions:

- **a)** Is anyone committing an illegal offence?
- **b)** Are there any other risks being taken? What are they?

a) False; **b)** True; **c)** True; **d)** True; **e)** True; **f)** False; **g)** False; **h)** True; **i)** False; **j)** True.

The drug economy

When it comes to information and discussion about drugs, many people focus on laws controlling their sale and penalties for using them. However, the whole picture is far more complex. Sometimes we talk about a '**drug economy**'. The next activity explores the bigger picture of drugs; their supply, sale and use.

Source 2 A drugs' supply chain

AFGHAN HILL FARMER

You farm in a remote hill area of Afghanistan. You have to work hard to make a living to keep your young family. If you grow sugar beet or a similar crop, you will get a government subsidy – but even taking this into account your annual earnings would be £500 per year. If you grow opium poppies you can sell the raw opium for £200 per kilo. Farming this way you can earn £1500 per year. The only world you know is the Afghan mountains. You are not aware of what happens to the crop once it leaves your hands.

DRUG PRODUCER

You buy the crop from the hill farmers and process it to make pure heroin. You are proud of the quality of the heroin you produce; it is pure when it leaves you and not mixed with any other substances. Some producers do make more money by mixing in cheaper substances but you realise this could be dangerous for the user. You work hard and if caught could spend a lifetime in jail. What you buy from the farmer for £200 you sell to an international gang for £5000. You live a good life.

DRUG SMUGGLER

You can make £5000 per shipment for bringing a kilo of heroin through customs. The risk is very high if you are caught, but you like the excitement of finding new ways of smuggling. You believe you are providing a service and think people should be free to use or take what they like.

DRUG SUPPLIER (DEALER)

You run a group of street suppliers who buy the heroin from you and sell it on to users. You believe people should be free to choose how they spend their money and if some want to use it to buy heroin you will supply it. You can make £80,000 profit on a kilo of heroin when it is sold, broken down into small 'bags'. You believe you help poor poppy farmers make a living.

HEROIN USER

You were introduced to heroin by a friend. You liked the effect. Now you have become dependent on it and need it regularly to keep going. You spend a lot of time working to get the money to buy supplies. You have your troubles in life and heroin seems to take away the worries. You would actually like not to be dependent on it but stopping is hard. You think you are harming nobody but yourself. You make sure that you always use clean injecting equipment that you don't share with anyone else.

ACTIVITY

Drugs – who is most responsible?

5. a) Split into five groups. Each group should take one of the characters in Source 2 and do the following:

- Prepare a case for your character in order to justify their place in the drugs trade and argue that they are not responsible for the drugs problem. You can go beyond the information above to give the character more appeal; for example, you can bring in details of families or friends ... or anything that will make the character more sympathetic.
- Choose someone who will take the role of the character and present their case for two minutes, as if in court.

b) After each character has spoken, take a class vote on whether they can see the point of view of your character and whether they sympathise with you.

c) After each character has spoken and been voted on, discuss who is the most responsible for keeping the drugs trade going.

ACTIVITY

A piece of advice

6. Imagine you have the opportunity to offer the government one piece of advice to help reduce the negative effects of drugs. What would it be and why did you choose it?

Based on an activity originally published in 'DrugWise', ISDD/SCODA/TACADE, 1986

Alcohol

In this topic you will learn about:

- minimising risks from alcohol use
- legislation on alcohol use.

You will explore:

- different views about young people's alcohol use
- sources of local help and support.

Suggested limits have been put in place to enable people to make healthy choices about how much alcohol they consume:

- Men — maximum 3–4 units per day
- Women — maximum 2–3 units per day
- Teenagers — under 15 years – none; over 15 years – infrequently; see below.

In December 2009 Professor Sir Liam Donaldson, the Chief Medical Officer for England, recommended that:

- children should have an alcohol-free childhood – if children drink alcohol, it shouldn't be before they are 15 years old
- if young people aged 15 to 17 years old drink alcohol, it should always be with the guidance of a parent or carer or in a supervised environment
- if young people aged 15 to 17 drink alcohol, they should do so infrequently and on no more than one day a week – they should never drink more than the adult daily limits recommended by the NHS.

www.direct.gov.uk/en/Nl1/Newsroom/DG_183393

ACTIVITY

Over the limit?

1. Using the illustration in Source 1, what could the following groups drink in a week and still stay within the recommended maximum?

a) men
b) women
c) teenagers

Source 1 How many units?

The law relating to underage drinking is intended to prevent people under 18 buying alcohol (see page 28). However, underage drinking is common, and the parent in Source 2 is struggling to decide what to do about her daughter's request.

Source 2

Parent to Parent – This week:

Is giving 15-year-olds alcohol at a party OK?

The question is followed by responses from other readers.

My daughter wants me to provide alcohol at her fifteenth birthday party. I plan to check with her friends' parents but her dad and I aren't sure it is appropriate. If we decide to go ahead, how much and what kind of alcohol is OK? We thought maybe a glass or two each and after that soft drinks?

'I'd let them have a glass of sparkling wine each and then soft drinks afterwards. I don't think you should be encouraging under-age teenagers to drink.' SW

'What if a few parents say OK but the majority are appalled at your suggestion? Your daughter is still a child and needs to be given a clear message that alcohol is not good for children – and isn't particularly good for adults either.' AS

'You should lay down the law. This will give your daughter the opportunity to say 'Tsk! Parents! They SO don't understand' but at the same time she can secretly be relieved and not lose face.' TP

'For my 16-year-old son's birthday party I provided jugs of non-alcoholic punch laced with angostura bitters to make it taste drier and different, as well as a variety of soft drinks. All those who came along focused on the food and having a good time and went home happy.' AB

'I'd say no. Chances are some of them won't want a drink – after all they are only 15. Adults don't help by providing opportunities where they may feel pressured to drink because their friends are doing so. If you provide the booze they will feel they *have* to drink it to avoid looking childish in front of their friends.' CF

'I can never remember a time when my parents didn't allow me at least a sip of alcohol – but they never provided it for my friends. You really have to check with all the other parents. If they are OK I'd limit it to one alcoholic drink each. This is your home – you have every right to set a limit. Remember, you can't control what they choose to do outside your home.' SA

Based on the 'Family Forum' column in the *Saturday Guardian*, 9 February 08

ACTIVITY

Party, party!

2. Look at Source 2. Which of the responses do you:

a) most agree with?
b) least agree with?

Give reasons to explain your answers.

c) Try writing a response that reflects your views.

ACTIVITY

More than health risks

3. Most people think of the risks associated with misusing alcohol as health risks; for example, liver disease and mental health problems. However, it poses risks for other things as well. Give examples of negative effects alcohol has for each of the following:

a) family
b) the law
c) employment
d) finance
e) social relationships.

ACTIVITY

Drink problems

4. Most areas have local organisations that people can turn to if they need help and support with alcohol-related problems.

a) Find out what local support groups exist in your area, what they do and how they can be accessed. The NHS has a directory that lists local alcohol addiction support groups (www.nhs.uk/servicedirectories).

b) Use the information you find to produce a poster for your school's PSHE notice board about local alcohol support groups and the service they provide.

Alcohol and the law

Source 3 Legislation about alcohol

1872 Licensing Act
Made it an offence to be drunk while in charge of carriages, horses, cattle and steam engines.

1898 Inebriates Act
Prevention of sale of alcohol to habitual drunkards.

1930 Road Traffic Act
Made it an offence to drive whilst being 'under the influence of drin[k] or a drug to such an extent as to be incapable of having proper control of the vehicle'.

2001 Criminal Justice and Police Act
- On-the-spot penalties for a range of offences including public drunkenness, disorderly behaviour whilst drunk in a public place and consumption of alcohol in a designated alcohol-free zone.
- Local authorities have power to designate public places as alcohol-free zones.
- Allows 'test purchasing' of alcohol – under-18s being used by police to test the willingness of licensees to sell illegally to the underage.

2003 Licensing Act
An offence is being committed if:
- under-18s buy or try to buy alcohol
- over-18s buy alcohol on behalf of under-18s (this does not apply if the child is 16 or over and is bought beer, wine or cider by someone aged 18 or over, but only to drink with a meal in the dining or restaurant area of a pub when accompanied by someone aged 18 or over)
- an under-18 is sent to buy alcohol on your behalf.

Because alcohol causes health problems as well as wider problems for society, the government has created laws about its use in order to try and minimise the harm it can cause. Legislation about alcohol has been developed over many years to address:

- the prevention of crime and disorder
- public safety
- the prevention of public nuisance
- the protection of children from harm.

Source 3 shows the timeline of some laws related to alcohol.

ACTIVITY

More laws?

5. What problems do you think brought about the need for the laws in the timeline in Source 3? In groups, choose one law and discuss reasons why you think this law was passed. Feed back your reasons to the class.
6. Alcohol consumption and problems associated with it still appear to be increasing. Do we need more legislation? The ideas in speech bubbles on the following page are all possible areas for new legislation about alcohol. Give an example of an argument for and against each.
7. Are there any other realistic and more workable solutions (other than more legislation) to reduce the problems associated with alcohol consumption?

1967 Road Safety Act
Introduced the first legal maximum blood-alcohol (drink-driving) limit in the UK and the breathalyser.

1974 Health and Safety at Work Act
Anyone under the influence of drink at work who endangers the health and safety of themselves or others is liable to prosecution.

Football Matches
Acts in 1980 and 1985 created offences including:

- being in possession of alcohol on the way to matches
- trying to enter a ground when drunk or in possession of alcohol
- possessing or consuming alcohol within view of the pitch during the period of the match
- being drunk during the period of the match.

a) Set a minimum price for alcohol to reduce sales to young people.

b) Supermarkets to stop multi-buy/bargain deals of cheap alcohol.

c) Reduce hours that pubs and clubs can open and sell alcohol.

d) Total ban on consuming alcohol on the street/in public places/on public transport.

e) Restrict happy hours or irresponsible price-based promotions; for example, women 'drink for free' promotions are still all too common.

f) Restrict the way alcohol is sold, such as offering drinks in small as well as large glasses or measures; for example, too often only one size is offered or a large is automatically given.

g) Display alcohol in designated and separate areas; for example, no more displays by the checkout.

1988 Cyclists: The Road Traffic Act
Made it an offence to cycle/ride a bike under the influence of drink or drugs.

1991 Road Traffic Act
Made it an offence punishable by a compulsory prison sentence to cause death by careless driving when under the influence of drink or drugs.

1997 Confiscation of Alcohol (Young Persons) Act
Gave police the power to confiscate alcohol from under-18s drinking in public places (streets, parks, etc.) and creating disorder.

ACTIVITY

The wisdom of Homer Simpson

8. Many people have made up witty sayings about alcohol – what's the message behind Homer's words: *'Beer. Now there's a temporary solution.'*?

Weighing up the pros and cons

In this topic you will learn about:

- definitions of positive and negative risks
- 'heart' and 'head' responses to risk.

You will explore:

- your personal responses to risk and risk-taking
- how different people perceive risk.

Source 1 What's the buzz?

What's the buzz?

1. Look at Source1. A young man is playing a game of chance. Discuss the following questions:
   a) Look at the expression on the young man's face. What words would you use to describe the 'buzz' he might be feeling?
   b) Why are games like this so mesmerising?
   c) Are there any risks or dangers associated with 'gaming'?

What is risk?

Every action that holds the possibility of a positive or negative outcome is a risk.

A **positive risk** is one where the intended outcome is beneficial to well-being; for example, sports, performing on stage, speaking in public, going for a job interview.

A **negative risk** is one where the undesired outcome damages well-being; for example, dependency on drugs and alcohol, carrying a weapon, exceeding the speed limit.

If you stop to think about it, every risk should involve weighing up:

- the probability or likelihood of something happening
- the impact or severity of the consequences.

Gambling is an example of a risk-taking activity. People think of gambling in different ways but it usually involves:

- two or more people, usually an operator and an individual
- risking a stake, usually money, on the outcome of a future event
- paying the stake by the loser to the winner.

In simple terms, gambling is any behaviour that involves risking money or valuables on the outcome of a game, contest or other event. This event or game may be totally or in part dependent on chance.

Source 2 Do you believe that ...

Gambling is addictive?

Gamblers are bad people?

Slot machines are harmless?

Scratch cards encourage people to gamble?

Gambling is a risk worth taking?

Online gambling is a mug's game?

ONLY IDIOTS GAMBLE?

ACTIVITY

Gambling is ...

2. In Source 2 there are some questions about gambling. What are your thoughts? Discuss the questions in groups.

ACTIVITY

Pushing your luck

3. You can be the world's greatest poker player, bingo babe or placer of bets – but if you can't manage your money you'll end up broke. What advice would you give to someone who was addicted to gambling?

Gambling is one type of risk-taking activity that can have serious consequences. In the next activity you will have the chance to think about other activities that have risks attached.

ACTIVITY

Rate the risk

4. Rank the following activities from 'totally safe' to 'extremely risky'.

- bungee jumping
- carrying a knife for protection
- drinking a bottle of spirits
- having unprotected sex
- playing fruit machines
- smoking cigarettes
- speaking in front of a group
- talking in internet chat rooms.

We are all individuals and have different attitudes to risk-taking. What for some of us might be a positive risk-taking experience might for others feel very negative and unsettling. We also have different attitudes to weighing up risks: some people will be very thoughtful and others will just jump in.

ACTIVITY

Thinking about you

5. a) What is the biggest negative risk you've ever taken?

b) Did you do anything to limit the potential for harm?

6. a) What's the biggest positive risk you've ever taken?

b) What did you gain from taking it?

7. Looking to the future, what positive risk would you most like to take?

a) What might stop you from taking that risk?

b) What would you gain from taking that risk?

8. On a scale of 1–10, how big a risk-taker would you say you are (with 1 as mega safe!)?

ACTIVITY

Obsessed?

9. Look at the young man in Source 1. If you are experiencing strong emotions (pleasure, fear, a 'buzz', etc.), does that make it harder or easier to weigh up the risks in any situation? Explain your answer.

3 Emotional and Mental Health

Recognising and balancing emotions

In this topic you will learn about:

- emotional health and how to recognise it
- the usefulness of personal support networks.

You will explore:

- the eight main types of emotions
- ways to expand social life and friendships.

ACTIVITY

Emotionally healthy?

1. If you were asked to describe a physically healthy person you could probably provide a good list of features; for example, eats a balanced diet, has good energy levels, etc. If you were asked to describe an emotionally healthy person, what would that list of features include?

Emotional health is as important as physical health, but we generally don't talk or hear about it in the same way. Recognising our range of emotions and learning how to keep them in balance is one way of opening up discussion about our emotional health.

There are different points of view about how many main emotions there are – but eight are universally recognisable, as shown in the photos below. Each of the eight could be called a 'main emotion', and within each of these there will be different degrees of feeling; for example, degrees of anger might include fury, annoyance, hostility, etc.

Source 1 The eight main emotions

Anger

Fear

Sadness

Enjoyment

Love

Disgust

Shame

Surprise

ACTIVITY

How do you know?

2. Look at Source 1, which identifies the eight main emotions.
   a) What characteristics in each facial expression represent the emotion?
   b) Can you identify a word that describes the degree of feeling being shown?
   c) Compare your answers with someone else – did you see similar degrees of feeling?
3. a) Choose one or two of the eight main emotions and create a collage of examples from photos, film or art that illustrate it. You could use the internet, magazines, books and films in your research.
   b) On your collage explain which emotion is represented by using evidence from the facial expression, tone of voice, body language, etc. In your explanation try and use different words to describe the degree of emotion being used. It may help to brainstorm these first.

Recognising and understanding our emotions is the first step in looking after our emotional health. The next step is to understand that being emotionally healthy isn't necessarily about feeling 'happy' all the time. Good emotional health will be about achieving balance and recognising when things are out of balance and how to restore equilibrium.

For example, it is natural to have some worries or concerns about all sorts of things, such as new or difficult tasks, upcoming examinations or unfamiliar social situations. But if the worries and concerns start to take over your thoughts and you find yourself constantly thinking about them or changing your daily routines to avoid them, then you may need to find a way of restoring the balance.

An example of one technique for restoring balance and achieving equilibrium is to know and use your 'personal support network'.

Source 2 A typical personal support network

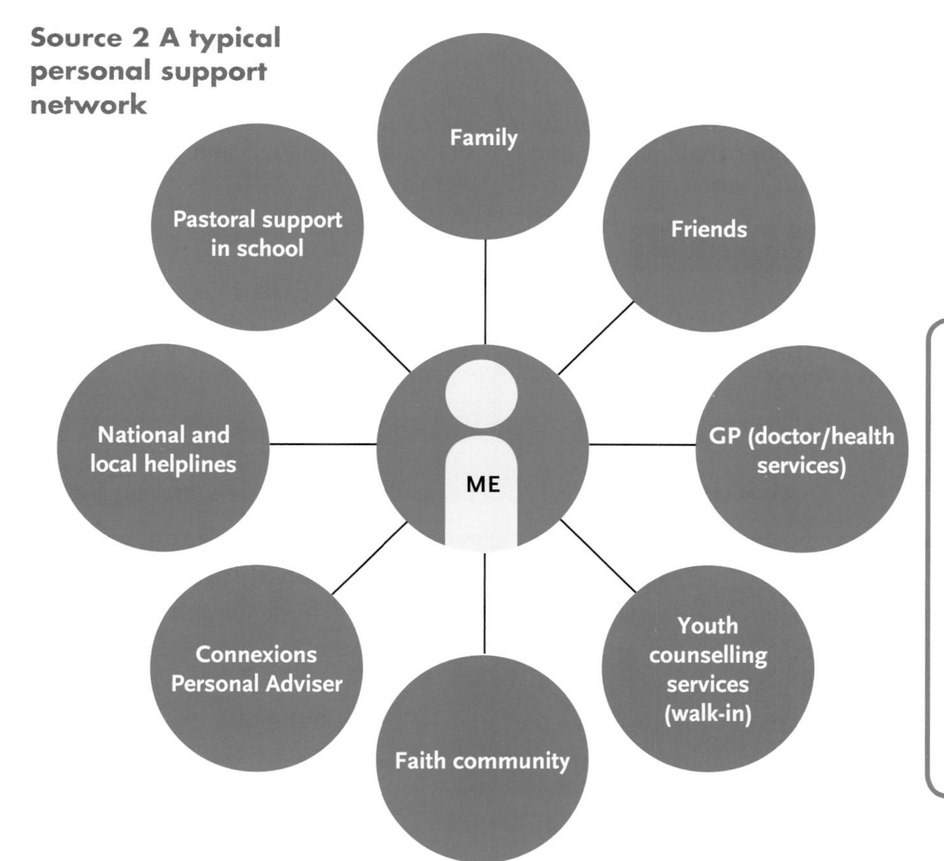

ACTIVITY

Who would I include?

4. Look at Source 2. Not everyone will have eight types of support on their personal network. What would be the two or three key strands that you would include on yours and why? Discuss your answer in pairs or small groups.

Friendship

Many people rely on friends for support, but some people find it difficult to make friends because they find it difficult to communicate. Source 3 gives some tips on how to communicate effectively.

Source 3

THE 5-POINT FRIENDSHIP PLAN

Some people make friends effortlessly. This isn't because they're any nicer or better than those who don't. It's because they know how to make conversation. If you feel like you never know what to say, this is for you.

1. Talk to everyone

What you say doesn't have to be original – it just has to be something! E.g. next time you buy something, say 'Thanks, have a good day'. Practice really does make perfect, so try to say something to everyone you meet.

2. Use body language

It's not just what you say, it's how you say it. If you seem approachable, friendly and relaxed, people will want to talk to you. How to do this? Make eye contact and smile.

3. Choose your friends wisely

At school there are cliques and tribes and everyone's supposed to know their place ... but there will also be people who are open to communication and new ideas and won't judge you. These are the people who often make the best friends.

4. Be a good listener

You don't have to be fascinating/beautiful/hilarious for people to want to talk to you. Listen to what people say, remember their names and their likes and dislikes, and just take the time to learn more about them.

5. Have the courage of your convictions

Don't say things you don't believe to make people like you. It won't work. Instead, believe in the value of your own opinions – and don't apologise for them. Having a good conversation doesn't mean everyone has to agree with everyone else.

www.bbc.co.uk/radio1/advice/factfile_az/problems_making_friends

ACTIVITY

Stepping stones

5. Discuss why each of the points in Source 3 is an important part of making and keeping friends.

6. If you knew someone who wanted to make more friends, or expand their social life, what steps other than those mentioned in Source 3 would you suggest they could take?

ACTIVITY

Emotional idol

7. Who is the most emotionally healthy person you know and what makes them so?

Stresses, pressures and exams

In this topic you will learn about:

- common physical and emotional signs of stress
- why good sleep habits are essential to managing pressures.

You will explore:

- ways of managing stress and anxiety
- recommended routines for dealing with exam pressures.

ACTIVITY

Coming to get you!

1. Imagine a scene from a science fiction film where a monster is chasing one of the characters. The character is unarmed and defenceless against the unremitting onslaught.
   a) How would they feel?
   b) What physical and emotional signs might signify that something scary was happening?

There is so much to deal with … one thing on top of another, such as:

ACTIVITY

If only there'd been more time

2. Most young people have different tips or techniques they use to reduce stress. What three methods to beat stress and anxiety would you pass on to a friend?

Sometimes it feels like everything's happening at once and that's stressful. But this stress doesn't have to pile up until it feels out of control. Taking time to acknowledge each issue and recognise what's happening can be helpful – so can being proactive and creating an action plan to use in those difficult times.

Sleep

One method of combating stress and anxiety is to make sure you get enough sleep in order to function well during the day. However, as Source 1 illustrates, sleep can be a problem for some young people.

Source 1 Sleep facts

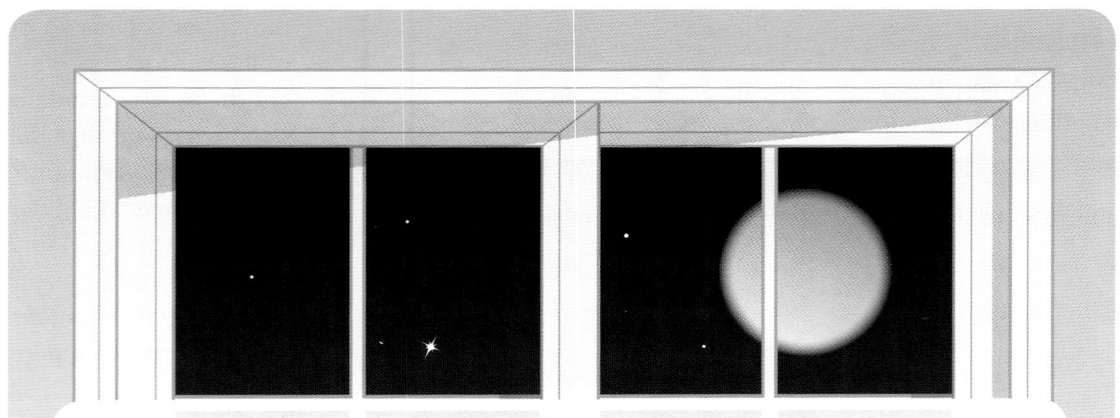

- 'Even though there is an epidemic of tiredness in society, people don't view sleep as a priority.' (Gordon Cairns, Govan High School in Glasgow)
- 'Sleep is crucial to repair, growth and the consolidation of knowledge and memory. It's no magic revelation.'(Jane Ansell, Director of Sleep Scotland)
- Two-thirds of children are not getting enough sleep, with some getting as little as five hours a night. They say they feel sleepy, but don't make the connection with the need to go to bed earlier.
- Going into bedrooms at a decent time is not sufficient if children stay awake for hours watching television, playing computer games, texting or surfing the internet.
- 'Media invasion has a severe social and neurological impact. Flash images from the computer, TV or mobile phone screens interfere with the body's production of melatonin, a chemical that helps trigger drowsiness.' (Mandy Gurney, Millpond Sleep Clinic, London).
- Sleep is a learned behaviour. Just as there have been improvements in healthy eating behaviours, so good sleep habits can become the norm.

ACTIVITY

Zzzzzzzzzzz

3. Most sleep advisers recommend that in order to get a good night's sleep you should follow a routine of winding down before bedtime, and that bedtime should be calm without too much stimulation. Use the outline to the right to create a plan that will lead to a good night's sleep and help combat some of the problems outlined in Source 1.

TIME	ACTIVITY
Arrive home from school	
Two hours before sleep time	
One hour before sleep time	
Sleep time	Get into bed and go to sleep!

Exam pressures

In this topic so far you have thought about ways to deal with stress/anxiety and also to improve sleep habits. Now it's time to address the big one – exams! Source 2 gives some suggestions for preparing for exams and keeping stresses at bay.

Source 2 What works best?

	IDEA	SCORE OUT OF 10
1	**Design an exam calendar** Use large squares for each day of the month and write down the dates of upcoming exams. Work out and plan how much preparation time is available.	
2	**Display each month's calendar page on the refrigerator** It will remind you to study a little each day and your family can refer to it as needed to offer you help and support leading up to the exam.	
3	**Don't just cram before the exam** The brain can only absorb so much information in a 24-hour period. Waiting until the last minute to cram for the test will just make the stress and pressure worse.	
4	**Use quotes, photos and music for inspiration** For example: 'Your entire future is not riding on one test.' 'Forget past mistakes. Forget failures. Forget everything except what you're going to do now and do it.' 'I'm not telling you it is going to be easy – I'm telling you it's going to be worth it.'	
5	**When you get into the exam room – don't panic** Read the instructions carefully. Scan the questions before beginning. Work out how long it will take to answer each one.	
6	**Think how you'll use your time** Consider answering the questions you have a solid command of first but don't forget to allow time and then go back to answer the others.	
7	**You can control your nerves** If you find yourself tensing up, getting clammy hands, or if your mind suddenly goes blank, close your eyes and slowly count to four until the stress eases. You may have to do this two or three times.	
8	**Talk about how you're feeling** Open up about your worries and allow others an opportunity to give you ideas on how you might overcome the stress. Remember you don't have to do everything that everyone suggests – but they may have ideas you haven't thought of.	
9	**Get plenty of sleep** Recent research from The National Centre on Sleep Disorders says that teenagers should get at least nine hours sleep a night. They found that 17-year-olds were only sleeping for 6.9 hours, affecting their performance in school.	
10	**Eat a healthy breakfast before taking the exam** Sensible eating keeps the brain alert and energy levels up.	

ACTIVITY

Pulling it all together

4. Look at Source 2. What do you think of the suggestions for preparing for exams and keeping stresses at bay? Score each suggestion out of 10, with 10 being 'yes, that really works' and 1 being 'not much use'.

ACTIVITY

Top tip

5. What is your top tip for facing stresses and pressures in the weeks leading up to examinations?

Money stresses and pressures

In this topic you will learn about:

- money – borrowing and interest
- risks attached to buying on credit.

You will explore:

- emotional and financial costs of misusing money
- solutions to financial problems.

Money, money, money

1. Everyone needs money in some shape or form. Using money can be a positive experience but misusing money has risks attached. Look at Source 1. Of all these different ways that a teenager might use money, which one might cause the biggest problems and why?

Source 1

Teenagers and money

The key financial life-stage experiences of most pupils between the ages of 11 and 16 include:

- using a savings account
- managing an allowance and gift income
- mobile phone tariffs
- opening a bank account
- using a debit card or pre-payment card
- use of e-commerce
- earnings from part-time employment
- independent travel
- buying clothing, small gifts, etc.
- selling goods.

My Money, www.pfeg.org

Part of becoming an independent adult is learning how to manage money. This starts with the situations that teenagers might face in Source 1, but money worries usually increase as we get older. On pages 39–40 are three case studies that describe typical problems that adults face in managing their finances.

ACTIVITY

The cost of money

2. Read the three case studies on pages 39–40 and answer the questions that follow them.

Case study 1: Sheila, Sam and Kirsty

Sheila is a single parent who lives with Sam, 15 and Kirsty, 13. She is a generous mum who enjoys buying gifts for her children and indeed for herself. She rents her home and doesn't manage to save anything – there is no money left at the end of each month. A lot of the time Sheila lives on her **credit cards** – she never manages to pay off more than the minimum monthly requirement. The children aren't aware of this and are used to having whatever they ask for.

Cutbacks at Sheila's place of work mean that many staff are faced with the possibility of **redundancy**. Sheila has only been with the company for four years so if she loses her job she won't get a big redundancy pay-out.

On the same day that she hears that 50 per cent of employees may need to be made redundant, she also receives her latest credit card statements. She owes about £5500 in total to three different credit card companies. She knows she is going to have to change her spending habits. What is worrying her even more is how to break this news to Sam and Kirsty. She knows they won't be happy about how this will affect them but what can she do?

Questions

a) What kind of things might Sheila have bought using credit cards?
b) Sheila feels that she has lost control – why is this the case?
c) How do you think Sam and Kirsty will react to the news their mother is going to give them? What will they be most worried about?
d) Sheila decides she must talk about 'needs versus wants' with Sam and Kirsty. What does this mean?
e) What could each member of the family do to improve the situation?

Case Study 2: Rafik

Rafik is 22 and is now living back at home with his parents after completing his university degree. He is not yet earning enough to have to start paying back his **student loan** from university days. He has a job assisting a local charity. It is not well paid, but he enjoys it.

Rafik has a lively social life with all his cousins and a great group of friends. They enjoy socialising and he enjoys looking good and keeping up with fashionable trends – clothes, phones, music, etc. Rafik has run up **debts** of almost £7000, mainly with several **store cards**, and he is only able to make the minimum payments on these. The store cards charge a high rate of interest and his debt is building every month. It had seemed so easy to get **credit** at the time – all you had to do was fill in a form and you didn't have to pay for it all straight away. Some of the shops even offered a massive discount on the day you signed up to their card. He hadn't realised that the interest rate (called the **APR** or Annual Percentage Rate) was much higher than the bank would have charged on an **overdraft**. Rafik now owes much more than he originally spent.

Rafik saw a documentary about people and debt on TV. He decided to contact a **money adviser** (a free service). He could then work out how to pay off his debts, although he knew it would take a long time. After talking his problems through, he has learned how to budget and has taken on a second job so that he can clear his store card debts more quickly and start to think about how he will pay off his student loan.

Questions

a) What kind of shops offer store cards?
b) How big a factor in building up his debt was the need to keep up with others?
c) How might huge debts impact on Rafik's emotional health?
d) What suggestions for improving his situation would Rafik have received when he used the free financial advice service?
e) How does someone judge between what is promoted as a 'good deal' and what they can really afford? What pros and cons do they have to consider?

Case study 3: Summer

Summer is 32 and single. She has a mortgage on her duplex apartment in a nice part of town. She works as a dental nurse and after monthly deductions (income tax, national insurance and pension contribution) her take home pay is £1250. When the dental practice was busy (before the recession) she earned even more through working later in the evenings and over the occasional weekend. Even though Summer earns less money now she has kept to her previous lifestyle. She has done this by using credit cards and now owes £17,000 spread over many different cards. She likes to eat out with friends, Friday night is 'girls' night out' and she always has the latest mobile phone and takes whatever contract she is offered in the shop.

With the situation at work not improving Summer realised she couldn't afford to carry on living at that rate. After seeing an advert on television she decided to take out a **secured consolidation loan** of £18,000. This paid off all her credit cards and put all her debts into one place. However, in order to secure the loan she had to tie it to her apartment as a guarantee.

To keep the monthly payments as low as possible, she took out the loan over 20 years at a monthly repayment of £150. However, Summer continued to spend as though nothing had changed and missed some payments on her loan. She took out a few new store cards to cheer herself up.

Summer hadn't looked at the small print of the loan and didn't realise that because she'd borrowed over 20 years at an APR of about 8 per cent, over the total time of the loan she would actually have to pay back over £35,000. With that and her new store cards, she built up a total debt of over £45,000 as well as having to pay her mortgage. She could not afford to keep up her payments and **defaulted on her mortgage**.

By the time Summer sought professional money advice it was too late and she was advised to go bankrupt. She lost her apartment – it was **repossessed** – and she had to start again, only this time she won't be able to get a mortgage or a loan, or use credit or store cards for the next year.

Questions

a) Summer saw an advert offering to consolidate all her loans into one. She thought it seemed too good to be true. Was it?

b) Spending to cheer yourself up (retail therapy) is not unusual. In Summer's case it cost more than she had bargained for. How might spending beyond her means affect her emotions and relationships with others?

c) Summer responded to a TV advert offering what looked like a good loan. Why might shopping around for the most appropriate financial products and services be a more sensible solution?

d) If you don't understand the financial implications of living independently (without parental support) where would you go for help and advice?

Source 2 Lottery win

Bus driver Kevin Halstead drove the 125 bus on the same route from Bolton to Preston for 17 years before winning £2.3 million on the lottery. In this photo he and his partner Josephine Jones celebrate their win. When he won he said he wouldn't quit his job because he would miss his colleagues. It seems money can't buy you friends, or happiness.

ACTIVITY

Money can't buy you happiness

3. Look at Source 2. What costs nothing and brings *you* happiness?

Work-life balance

In this topic you will learn about:

- common stresses experienced by teenagers
- strategies for time management.

You will explore:

- the concept of a work–life balance
- other people's attitudes to work and personal happiness.

ACTIVITY

It's such a hassle!

1. 124 teenagers were asked in a survey to talk about what stressed them the most. The topics they came up with (in alphabetical order) were:

- Family/parents
- Managing time
- School/homework
- Social life
- Sports

Which of these do you think was mentioned most and which least? Put the five in the order you think they occurred – from most to least mentioned as the main source of stress. (Answers below.)

ACTIVITY

Work–life balance

2. What strategies would you recommend to a friend who felt stressed or overwhelmed when trying to manage their time and commitments? Use Source 1 to help you.

The phrase 'work–life balance' has become quite common. One way of explaining this idea is to see it as balancing the amount of time you spend doing your job compared with the amount of time you spend with your family and doing things you enjoy.

Achieving the right work–life balance may sound like something that will affect you in the future. However, although right now you may not be holding down full-time jobs, you may still feel under a lot of pressure from daily responsibilities. Everyone can benefit from finding a healthy balance rather than having a life that feels like a juggling act. Could managing our time more efficiently be a key way to achieve a better balance (see Source 1)?

Source 1

Prioritising – time management for students

When there seems to be a million things to do, prioritising can seem difficult. It is important to look at which activities or projects will take longest, which are hardest and which are due or are happening soonest.

- Work out a balance between school and other activities that makes sense for you, and set an amount of time for each activity.
- Make a list of what you have to do, and when you have to have it done.
- Cross out or check off what you have done.
- Decide how much time you want to spend on each item on your to-do list.
- Break up bigger projects into more manageable parts; for example, with an assignment, you can start with finding sources, then taking notes, then doing an outline, writing a rough draft and then editing and proofreading. This way, you don't have to do it all at once.
- Plan what times you want to set aside for work, and what time you have for other activities (study after breakfast, take a break for lunch, play a sport for one hour, study until dinner, then relax for the night and get a good night's sleep so you can focus the next day).

The Palo Alto Medical Foundation for Health Care, Research and Education

Most to least mentioned: School/homework; Family/parents; Social life; Managing time; Sports.

Finding out more

3. Some people spend so much time working that they don't notice that they're missing out on time for themselves and the people who matter to them.

a) Use the quiz in Source 2 to interview three people who are working. It will help them identify how healthy their work–life balance is.

b) Feed back your findings to the class and then discuss the following questions:

- The British workforce has a reputation for not taking a lunch break that gives them an opportunity to rest and refresh. Did your results confirm this?
- Did you spot any common factors or experiences amongst people who felt they had a good work–life balance?
- People can get very excited, passionate and involved in work – but can this be detrimental to the rest of their lives?
- Should one live to work, or work to live?

Source 2

A work–life quiz

1. When you are not actually at work or travelling to it, how often do you think or worry about work?
(a) I don't (c) Once a week
(b) Not very often (d) Most days
(e) It's always on my mind

2. How many hours a week do you spend at work and travelling to work?
(a) Less than 39 (d) 60–69
(b) 40–49 (e) More than 70
(c) 50–59

3. How often do you make sure your lunch break lasts more than half an hour?
(a) Every day (d) Only if I'm able to
(b) Most days (e) Lunch? What's that?
(c) Once a week

4. How often does pressure of work stop you enjoying time with your family or your friends?
(a) Never! Family comes first
(b) Not very often
(c) More often than I would like
(d) All the time
(e) Friends? There's no time for friends.

5. Does work ever have a negative effect on the rest of your life?
(a) No – it's only a job
(b) Not very often
(c) Often
(d) All the time
(e) I have no life outside work

6. Do you ever feel tired or depressed because of work?
(a) No – it's only a job
(b) Not very often
(c) Often
(d) All the time
(e) Too tired to be depressed

7. Does work ever make you feel worried, anxious or upset?
(a) No – it's only a job
(b) Not very often
(c) Often
(d) All the time
(e) No time to be anxious

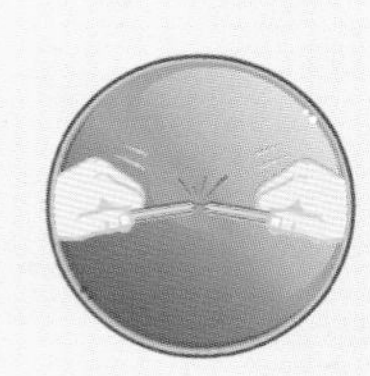

(Answers below.)

Mostly (a) and (b): You have a fair work–life balance; **Mostly (b) and (c):** You are not doing badly – but make sure you keep some time for yourself; **Mostly (c) and (d):** You need to look at your work–life balance in some areas; **Mostly (d) and (e):** You need help in sorting out your work–life balance.

Dividing my time

4. Here are five things that can compete for your time:

- family; • me-time; • education/school;
- friends/social life; • physical recreation.

Do you have an even balance of the time you spend on them?

Facing challenges

In this topic you will learn about:

- strategies that can be used when facing new challenges
- the meaning of 'empathy'.

You will explore:

- how to take an empathetic approach to problem-solving
- how you can apply problem-solving approaches to your own situations.

Facing new challenges

YES or NO?

1. Are you feeling confident about the challenges you will be facing in the next two years?

As you change from pupil to student to adult you will continually face new opportunities and obstacles that may, at first, seem impossible to overcome. However, through both creative and logical processes and looking at things in different ways, you can triumph. Sources 1–3 show some strategies for facing challenges.

Source 1 My view, your view, their view

This asks you to look at three ways of seeing a situation: my view, your view and the view of a detached observer. These are three different perceptual positions.

For example, let's say you are disagreeing with another person. It might help to mentally run through these three perceptual positions.

- The first position is to assess your own view of how you are feeling.
- Next imagine you are the other person and consider what the situation is from their point of view. Recognise how they might be feeling.
- Finally go into the third perceptual position. This time look at what is happening from the viewpoint of a detached and objective onlooker, recognising what is going on between these two people. Are they communicating with each other or are they more interested in doing things their own way?

Going through these three viewpoints (perceptual positions) will provide you with valuable information which, if you choose, can enable you to re-think your approach. If a person can put aside the 'me, me, me' attitude it can make communication and problem-solving better and happier for everyone involved.

Source 2
The Four Cs

You might remember this from previous work in PSHE Education.

When facing any challenge, here are four steps that can help a person choose what is right for them. Each person should try to achieve a positive outcome for anyone else involved in facing this challenge.

1. **Clarify** the issue
2. **Consider** the problem
3. Identify the **consequences**
4. **Choose** the most appropriate course of action.

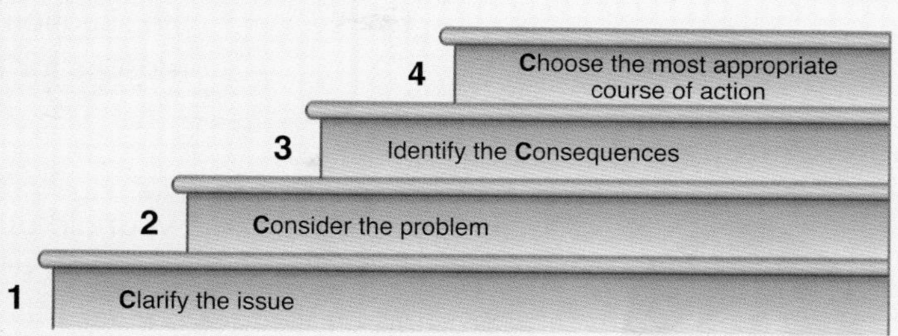

Source 3
SUMO

SUMO is Latin for 'I choose'. If you are wrestling with life's challenges, SUMO can help you do so more successfully.

SUMO encourages you to use specific phrases to remind you how to handle challenges and move forward. SUMO can be summarised by six principles:

1. Change your T-Shirt
Take responsibility for your own life by rejecting labels such as 'Nerd', 'Victim', 'Loser', etc.

2. Develop fruity thinking
Make your thinking positive – think of a half-full glass, not a half-empty one. Focus on solutions, not problems.

3. Hippo time is OK
Everyone needs time to wallow – take time to look after yourself if you feel under pressure. But be careful not to wallow for too long.

4. Remember the beach ball
Different views can be equally valid, just as the colours you can see on a beach ball depend on where you are standing when you look at it.

5. Learn Latin
In other words 'Carpe Diem' – seize the day – take positive action, and don't put things off until tomorrow.

6. Ditch Doris Day
Reject the 'Whatever Will Be Will Be' sentiment of Doris' song 'Que Sera Sera' – take action to create the future you want.

SUMO could be summed up as 'Shut Up Move On' – in other words shut up the negative voice inside you that undermines your confidence. Then you will be more able to move on and achieve your goals.

You can find out more about SUMO at www.thesumoguy.com.

Will these work?

2. Look at Sources 1 to 3 and discuss whether these approaches to facing challenges would be useful. What are the advantages and disadvantages of the different approaches?

Problem-solving

3. Read Sources 4–7 and consider the different challenges each person is facing. Which of the three approaches in Sources 1–3 (pages 44–45) would help them to manage the situation and their feelings surrounding it? Explain your reasons for each.

Source 4 Robert, 17

I take care of my 15-year-old autistic brother and also my mother who has cancer. My brother attends a special day school and looking after him presents challenges because he has a mental age of about six or seven. His behaviour can be fairly off the wall and unpredictable. As well as supporting my mum through her illness I take responsibility for dealing with letters, bills, phone calls and appointments because English isn't my mum's first language. My day usually starts at 5.30am and ends at 11pm. I don't know where to begin to start making things better or what course of action to take.

Source 5 Chanelle, 16

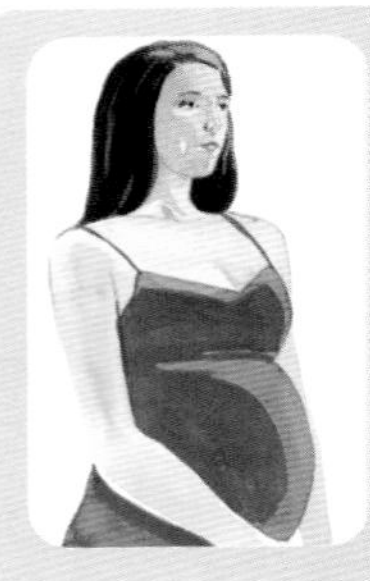

When I found out I was pregnant I was terrified. My mum got over it really quickly and is supportive. But my dad didn't talk to me for ages. He really disapproves of what I've done. He wants me to have the baby adopted. He says we can't afford another mouth to feed. He's lost his job and money is tight. If he's at home all day why can't he look after the baby while Mum is at work and I'm at school?

Source 6 Mac, 22

My family life broke down years ago – when we became homeless. I've been getting into trouble since I was 13. When I needed food or somewhere to sleep, I started breaking the law. My crimes got worse as I got older. The last prison sentence I received was when I was 17. I was given six years for robbery, theft and blackmail. I've been in several prisons and while I was inside I got all sorts of job qualifications. Now I'm 22 and I've been out of prison for seven months, yet I'm being punished every day – I thought my sentence was over. As an ex-offender I'm discriminated against and can't find a job.

Source 7 Rachel, 15

Walking home from school every day I think about what I have to come home to and it plays on my mind. My mother recently re-married. My dad lives abroad. My stepfather has started making things up to get me grounded. He winds me up so he has an excuse to have a go at me. Once when I told him where to go he grabbed me in front of my stepsister. I felt really humiliated. She shouted at him but he told her to leave the room. I went upstairs, put my face in the pillow and screamed with sadness. I do worry – but what's the point? I know what I want in life, I just wonder if I'll get there.

At different stages in our lives we are faced with new challenges and making difficult choices – often these relate to money.

ACTIVITY

In their shoes

4. a) Sheila has a limited income and is living off her state pension. She can't afford all of these so which do you think Sheila should spend her money on?

Afternoon at the pool with friends

Council Tax (a legal requirement)

Repair cost of broken TV

Birthday present for her grandchild

Packet of cigarettes

Soap, shampoo

Food for the weekend

Posed by model

Pet food

Overdue electricity bill

b) Now reflect on this activity:

- Was it easy to make decisions for Sheila?
- What were the difficulties in prioritising her wants and needs?

c) Use your empathy skills to re-write the expenses in a), imagining it is a list of nine financial demands on the parents of teenagers.

ACTIVITY

Facing future challenges

5. Reflect back to when you chose options in Year 9 – or forward to what you will do after your GCSEs. These were and will be big challenges and opportunities. In the next few months you are likely to face a challenge or two. What might these be and which of the strategies you have learned about would you use and why?

Bereavement

In this topic you will learn about:
- numbers of people affected by bereavement
- a model to explain the feelings experienced in bereavement.

You will explore:
- a lyrical response to bereavement
- ways to support a bereaved person.

Source 1 Bereavement and ritual

Burying a dead pet

Military funeral of a soldier killed in Afghanistan, 2010

Headstone of a grave in a Jewish Cemetery – the stones are placed by visitors who remember the dead person

> **ACTIVITY**
>
> **Early experiences**
>
> **1.** Most children's first experience of death is usually when a pet dies. They will often ask their parents to bury the dead pet in the garden and give it a 'funeral' service. What are the typical things a child might want to do at the pet's funeral?

> **ACTIVITY**
>
> **Marking a bereavement**
>
> **2.** The photos in Source 1 show different funeral rituals. Discuss why people feel the need to have such rituals around the death of someone or something they love.

Sooner or later in life each of us will probably experience bereavement and grief.

Being bereaved usually means that someone we love has died. When this happens people go through all sorts of changes that may affect them emotionally, physically, spiritually and socially. The impact on each person will be different – but most people will feel enormous pain, or sorrow.

Learning to live with this loss may take years. Each year it is estimated that in the UK:

- 20,000 children and young people under the age of 16 are bereaved of a parent
- 182,500 women become widows
- 175,000 men become widowers
- 12,000 children die.

Many others are affected by the death of a parent, a friend or a much-loved pet.

People will choose to mark death in different ways.

Source 2

The upward spiral of grief

People often share similar feelings following a bereavement: shock, despair, denial, anger, fear, guilt, anxiety, relief, sadness. It's important to know that these feelings are 'normal'.

'The Upward Spiral of Grief' is a way for people to understand and accept their feelings. Feelings may come back time and again and grieving is a long-term process.

For example, if six months after a loss someone still feels really tearful and sad one day, they may worry there's something wrong with them. However, they can stop and realise that they are now in a different place from the black hole they were in at the very beginning. Their feelings will be the same but with less intensity. They will have moved around the spiral and moved on, making some adjustments.

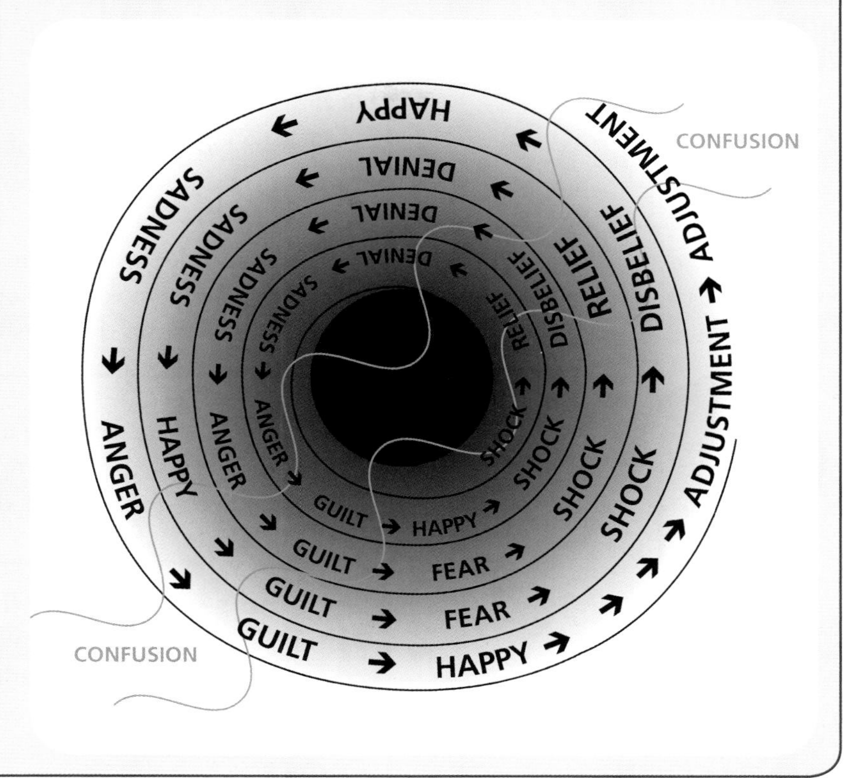

Different people express their grief in different ways. Eric Clapton, guitarist and singer-songwriter, expressed his grief at the loss of his child by writing *Tears in Heaven*.

Expressing feelings

4. Look up the lyrics of 'Tears in Heaven', especially lines 5–8. How do you interpret what Eric Clapton was trying to say?

Helping others to cope with bereavement

5. Some people find it difficult to know what to say when someone dies. They might be unintentionally thoughtless or unkind. Perhaps they just don't understand, are frightened or unaware. In groups, produce a small resource designed to help someone support a friend who is bereaved.

a) Choose the format of the resource (leaflet, pamphlet, webpage, etc.).

b) Research and decide what you would include to help the supportive friend. Use the websites listed below as a starting point:
www.griefencounter.org.uk
www.childhoodbereavementnetwork.org.uk/haad.htm
www.helpguide.org/mental/helping_grieving.htm

c) Create your resource.

Adjustment

ACTIVITY

3. 'Life will never be the same. It's different. And that's OK.' These are the words of someone who has experienced bereavement. Look at Source 2. How does it help to explain the feelings this person is going through?

Here and now

ACTIVITY

6. Sometimes when a loved one has died people say, 'I wish I'd told them how much they meant to me'. Choose someone alive now of whom you think a great deal. Create a one-line appreciation message to give them.

4 Relationships

Relating to others

In this topic you will learn about:

- different types and levels of relationships.

You will explore:

- the varied roles within your relationships
- the factors that make relationships successful or difficult
- the place of rights, responsibilities and respect in relationships.

Friends – fun ones and annoying ones!

Parents

Somone who is a good listener

In our daily lives we observe all sorts of relationships around us. Television dramas and soap operas show different relationships, as do films, books, music videos and advertisements.

Who's who in their lives?

1. List all the different relationships you have seen in films, TV, books and advertising. Use the photographs on these two pages to start you thinking about different types of relationships.

What about you?

2. a) Now thinking about yourself, what different types of relationships do you experience in your life? Using Source 1 as a guide, create your own relationship rainbow.
- Start with yourself in the middle and represent some of your relationships, with little drawings and/or names or initials, using distance from yourself to indicate the significance of the relationship.
- Put up to ten people in the diagram, and include both close and distant relationships, and good as well as difficult relationships.

b) Choose one person from your rainbow with whom you have a significant relationship and answer the following questions:
- What type of relationship is it (friend/family/work, etc.)?
- Why is it significant?
- What makes it a good relationship or what makes it difficult?

c) As a class discuss:
- Why are close relationships important?
- Are close relationships important to everyone?

Source 1 Relationships rainbow

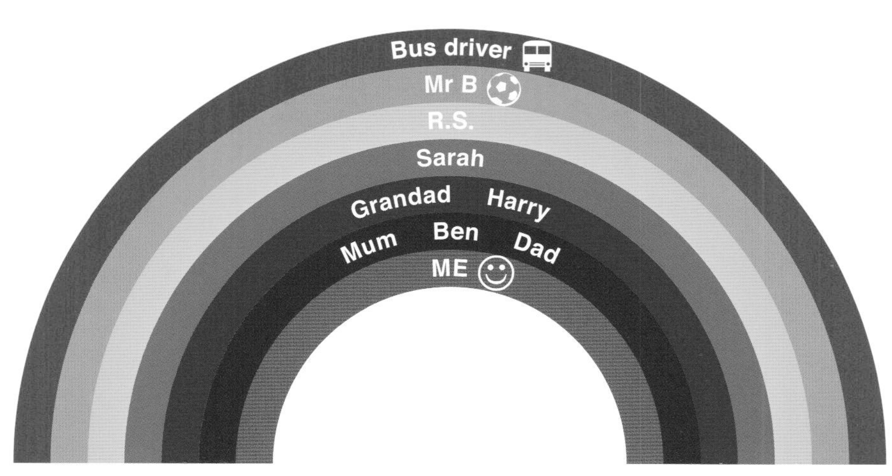

Shop and sales staff

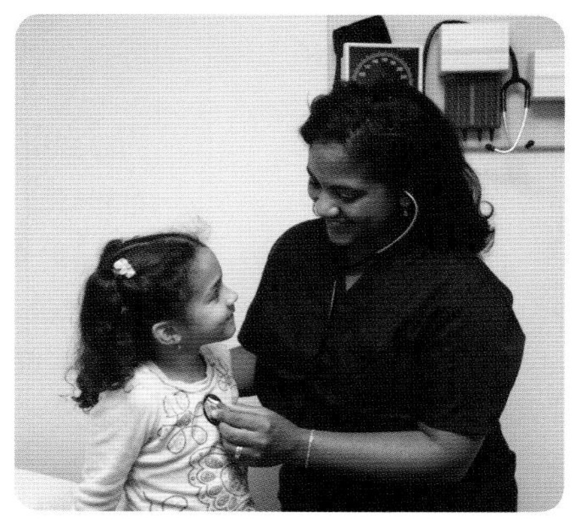

Professionals who help us – doctors, nurses, police, teachers, etc.

People we see around in the community

Sometimes we are fortunate and a good relationship just happens – you 'click' with someone. Most relationships, though, need working at and maintaining to help you and the other person relate well to each other.

Both people in a relationship need to think of their interaction as a combination of **rights and responsibilities**. These two concepts go together. At some level *every* relationship involves both rights and responsibilities.

Think about this everyday example:

If I'm waiting at the bus stop I have a right to expect the bus driver to stop, sell me a fare and look after my safety. I have a responsibility to pay my fare and behave safely and appropriately towards the driver and other passengers.

Relationships need work

3. Discuss the following questions:

a) What makes for a good relationship?

b) What might make a relationship difficult?

c) How important are 'rights and responsibilities' in a relationship? Can you give a similar example to the passenger and bus driver above?

d) A lot of young people say one of the most important elements of a relationship is 'respect'. What does that mean to you?

Relationships at work

4. People often overlook the fact that when they are at work they need good relationships. The people at work don't have to be your best friends, so why do you need to build good relationships with them?

Parenting skills and family life

In this topic you will learn about:
- the different ways that families operate
- the challenges of bringing up a family
- family budgeting.

You will explore:
- how different people interpret the word 'family'
- the skills needed to be a good parent
- ways that families can work together to manage money.

'A family is a unit composed not only of children but of men, women, an occasional animal, and the common cold.'

Ogden Nash, author and poet, 1902–1971

'When our relatives are at home, we have to think of all their good points or it would be impossible to endure them.'

George Bernard Shaw, playwright, 1856–1950

'Every family has a secret – that it is not like any other family.'

Alan Bennett, playwright, screenwriter and author, 1934–

'Call it a clan, call it a network, call it a tribe, call it a family. Whatever you call it, whoever you are, you need one.'

Jane Howard, children's books author

ACTIVITY

What can I say about family?

1. Each of the writers above has different feelings about 'family' – some funny, some cynical, some realistic. Write a couple of lines to express what you feel about 'family'.

A usual definition for family is a group of people who are related to each other. However, people who take part in communal activities such as those shown in Source 1 often describe their social group as 'their family'.

Source 1 A sense of family

ACTIVITY

What is family?

2. What do people mean when they call a social group they belong to their family?
3. How do the photos in Source 1 show characteristics of a family?

People may feel that family life gives them stability; knowing they can depend and rely on the people around them. Many people in relationships choose to have children. The Oxford English Dictionary defines this type of group as a **nuclear family**: 'a couple and their dependent children, regarded as a basic social unit'.

There are also plenty of families who would not fit this definition; for example, there are:

- extended families (including grandparents, aunts, uncles, cousins) who live together
- single-parent families
- step-parent families
- families that comprise people who live together and are not related in any way.

ACTIVITY

Types of family

4. Different family groups have different ways of behaving together:
   - authoritarian – there are clear, fixed rules about what is and what is not allowed
   - inconsistent – sometimes there are strict rules but at other times none
   - negotiating – there is dialogue between adults (parents) and teenagers, with the young people gradually gaining more autonomy.

   Name one advantage and one disadvantage for each of these.

Whatever the family type, there are some general key skills that many people say are important for being a good parent. Source 2 gives a list of these.

Source 2

Parenting skills

ASPIRING
Wanting their children to become the best they can be.

CONTROL AND DISCIPLINE
The ability to run the family fairly.

LOVE AND AFFECTION
Letting their children know they are loved.

MANAGING THE HOME
Budgeting, cleaning, clothing, feeding, etc.

PRAISE
Encouragement in all aspects of their children's lives.

RIGHT AND WRONG
Teaching their children a moral code to help them in life.

SAFETY
The skills to keep children safe from harm and risk.

TEMPER
Not to 'lose it' by being harsh or cruel.

TIME AND INTEREST
Spending time with their children: reading, playing, hanging out, etc.

ACTIVITY

Parenting skills

5. The list of parenting skills in Source 2 is in alphabetical order. Which would be your priorities? Use a diamond nine format as shown below and place the nine skills using position 1 for the most important. Remember that position 9 doesn't mean that skill has no importance.

1
2 3
4 5 6
7 8
9

What is good parenting?

6. a) Read Source 3. In light of what you have learned about key parenting skills, do you think these are examples of good parenting? Give reasons why/why not for each.

b) Now write a list of statements like those in Source 3 that describe a good child (teenager).

Source 3 Is this good parenting ... or not?

a) Always buying the latest gadgets/trainers/fashions for their children.

b) Being very strict about what time their children have to be back at home.

c) Checking out their children's friends.

d) Giving their children an allowance to spend each week – no strings attached.

e) Not allowing their child to drink alcohol until they are 18.

f) Expecting to know where their children are going to be when they go out.

g) Allowing their children lots of freedom to make mistakes.

h) Permitting their children to use illegal drugs at home, because it's safer than elsewhere.

Can the good parenting skills you have been looking at be taught? Source 4 shows an extract from an organisation's website that tries to do just that. Positive Parents offers advice on how to parent through books, podcasts, parenting-made-easy workshops and coaching.

Source 4

Parenting – the most natural thing in the world?

Hi, my name is Sue Atkins and I am the founder of Positive Parents. I know what it is like to be a parent. I am on that rollercoaster ride of negotiating, disciplining and communicating with my own teenage children, every day. I know how tough being a parent can be.

But I also know what a wonderful role it is too. As parents, you like me are the most important people in our children's lives.

And you deserve to have the right tools and techniques for your own family so you can have a happier home. Would you like to know how to:

- instantly reduce stress in your home
- get your children to follow your instructions without shouting at them
- feel like you and your partner are working together as a team
- have an easy and natural relationship with your child so they feel happy coming to you with problems and challenges they are facing
- have fun and laugh with your child
- feel more confident in your parenting decisions?

Well, now you can.

www.positive-parents.com

ACTIVITY

Born not made?

7. Why do you think organisations such as Positive Parents (see Source 4) might appeal to some parents?
8. There are different points of view about whether there should be some sort of parenting qualification. In order to drive a car you need a licence – should something similar be introduced before you can become a parent? Discuss reasons for and against it being introduced.

Part of good parenting is trying to manage the home well, including budgeting. One of the issues that can often cause conflict and arguments in a family is money: Who's bringing it in? Who's spending it? Is there enough to go around? Budgeting well and planning family finances may help avoid these sorts of conflict.

Source 5 Monthly financial planner

MONEY COMING IN	**£**		
Parent('s') take-home pay	3400		
Working children's contributions	125		
Other sources (savings, investments, etc.)	100		
Family allowance	135		
		TOTAL INCOME £	**3760**
MONEY GOING OUT	**£**		
BASICS	**£**	**LUXURIES**	**£**
Mortgage/rent	1000	Lunches/coffees (not home-made)	150
Council Tax	125	Eating out/social drinking	200
Gas	50	Outside entertainment, e.g. cinema	50
Electricity	30	Sport & recreation, e.g. gym, swimming, etc.	70
Water	20	Hair/beauty	100
Phone (bundle)	25	Home entertainment, e.g. CDs/DVDs	30
TV Licence	15	Satellite/cable subscription	20
Groceries	800	Magazines/newspapers	15
Clothing	150	Mobile phones	40
Babysitting	80	Lottery tickets/betting	10
Vehicle running costs	160	Vet's bills	25
Other travel costs	120	Gardening	15
Insurance (house/life/car, etc.)	50	Cleaner	80
Other, e.g. pocket money	50	Holidays	200
TOTAL BASICS EXPENDITURE £	**2675**	**TOTAL LUXURIES EXPENDITURE £**	**1005**
NON-MORTGAGE DEBTS	**£**		
Credit/store card repayments	65		
Loan repayments	70		
Other	–		
TOTAL NON-MORTGAGE DEBTS £	**135**		
		Total expenditure £	**3815**
		TOTAL INCOME minus TOTAL EXPENDITURE (£3760 – £3815)	**–£55 (DEBIT)**

ACTIVITY

Family budgeting skills

9. Look at Source 5, which shows a typical family budget planner. The areas listed are those that the family regularly spend on; and right now they're having difficulties managing. Offer some suggestions for where and how the family – including the children – could make savings.

ACTIVITY

Impacting on others

10. Most people could change one thing about their own behaviour to make life at home easier and happier with others. Assuming you're not perfect, what one thing would you change about yourself?
11. Imagine you had to write a postcard of appreciation to your parent/carer. What one thing would you most value them for?

When relationships go wrong

In this topic you will learn about:

- things that can make relationships unhealthy or damaging
- laws that support people in unhealthy relationship situations.

You will explore:

- how respect can be an important part of a relationship
- whether the PSHE curriculum should teach about current social problems.

This topic contains information on two areas where young people may be vulnerable in their relationships: grooming and domestic violence.

FACT FILE: GROOMING

What is it?
This is a process used by ill-intentioned adult(s) to befriend young people with the intention of abusing them. We often hear of it happening over the internet – but it can also occur within relationships.
It usually occurs in five stages:

1. Friendship
Flattering a young person to win their trust.

2. Forming a relationship
E.g. asking them what problems they have to create the illusion of being their best friend.

3. Risk assessment
In the case of the internet, asking them about the location of their computer and who else has access to it in order to assess the risk of being detected. Often the 'groomer' will get the adults that surround the child to accept and even welcome their involvement with the young person.

4. Exclusivity
Building up a sense of mutual love and trust, suggesting that they can discuss 'anything'.

5. Sex talk
Engaging the young person in explicit conversations and perhaps asking for inappropriate photos. At this stage the adult will usually try to arrange a meeting with the young person.

Who does it affect?
Anyone could be a victim of grooming. If the process takes place over the internet, the adult 'groomer' will often pretend to be a different gender/age, etc. in order to win trust.
A young person might be particularly at risk if they are:

- needy or crave attention – and enjoy the positive interest
- quiet – less likely to tell
- younger – less likely to understand or tell
- picked on by other children – so need a friend
- lacking in self-esteem – so vulnerable to the positive reinforcement from the 'groomer'
- eager to please
- unsupervised – vulnerable to the attention of the 'groomer'.

Why don't those who are affected do something about it?

- They may not realise it's happening. The 'groomer' will often lie and pretend to be younger than they are or someone other than themselves.
- They enjoy the attention and don't understand what is going on.
- They may not want to stop being 'friends' or let down their new friend.
- Usually when online young people are in their own homes and feel safe.

What does the law say?

- Online, if someone is being inappropriate – saying sexual things or asking you to do things that you feel are wrong – you have the right to save the conversation, block them and report it to CEOP (Child Exploitation and Online Protection Centre): www.ceop.gov.uk/reportabuse.
- It is a crime for anyone to meet (or even set up a meeting) with a child/young person if they are doing so for unlawful purposes.
- A person is breaking the law and acting as a 'groomer' if they put into place plans to meet a child/young person with the intent of having sexual contact.

Who can help?

CEOP

Police

Internet safety

As we have seen, one type of damaging relationship can come from an ill-intentioned adult grooming a young person over the internet. It is very important that people know how to use the internet safely in order to protect them from the risk of such relationships forming. Source 1 gives some examples of boundaries to set when using social networking sites in order to use them safely.

Source 1

Safe social networking

✓ Know your boundaries beforehand and decide what's acceptable to you and what isn't. Just because it's right for someone else it doesn't make it OK for you.

✓ Remember that people can turn. If you refuse to go along with anything that makes you feel uncomfortable you might see another side to your online 'friend'.

✓ If it doesn't feel right or your warning signals start buzzing, simply use the 'off' button. No one can force you to do anything you don't want to do.

✓ Don't let your cyber life take you over – yes it can be fun, but so can heaps of other things – so put a time limit on your cyber activity, and stick to it.

ACTIVITY

Good advice

1. Look at Source 1 and think back to other work you have done on internet safety. If you had to offer a younger sibling advice on this topic, what two do's and two don'ts would you suggest?

FACT FILE: DOMESTIC VIOLENCE

What is it?
Domestic violence is very common and can ruin people's lives. The police estimate that they get a call every minute from someone who is a victim of domestic violence. It can be described as threats, violence or abuse between people who have a relationship with each other (or have had in the past). Some people use the word 'abuse' instead of 'violence'. The terms are interchangeable.

One form of domestic violence is child abuse. This is when a child or young person is harmed, neglected or bullied by an older adult. A child/young person doesn't have to be physically hurt to be a victim of child abuse. If they are constantly being sworn at, teased or told that they are unwanted, this may also be classed as emotional abuse. Young people are also affected by witnessing domestic violence between adults in their homes.

Who does it affect?

Domestic violence can happen between partners and within families. It affects men and women in both straight and gay relationships and in all cultures and religions. It occurs all over the world regardless of wealth or geographical location.

It's based on one person having power or control over another. Physical violence is a common part of it – and this can include sexual assault – but it can take other forms such as psychological harm, emotional abuse or controlling someone's life financially or by restricting their freedom. Often it can start gradually – perhaps name-calling or threats – but it usually gets worse as time goes by.

Why don't those who are affected do something about it?
People often stay in the situation for many different reasons. They may be frightened to leave because they:

- worry the abuser will try and stop them and become even more violent
- rely on the abuser for financial support
- fear losing access to their children
- enjoy some parts of the relationship and keep hoping it won't happen again.

What does the law say?
It is a crime for anyone to attack you in your own home or elsewhere – whether they are your partner, a family member or someone you share your home with. Nobody has the right to abuse you in this way. You may be made to feel responsible and guilty for the abuse but the source of the problem is the abuser, not you.

Who can help?
Victim Support
Refuge Centres
Police

Source 2

Expect respect!

Awareness of abuse has often been focused on adults – but a recent NSPCC survey showed that a quarter of girls and 18 per cent of boys have experienced some sort of physical violence in a relationship from their partner.

Abuse in teenage relationships may involve:

- physical violence
- pressuring a partner into having sex
- controlling behaviour
- unnecessary jealousy or anger.

As we have seen, domestic violence can affect many people. Campaigners have put forward a proposal that students should learn more in PSHE on why domestic violence against girls and women is unacceptable. Source 3 gives some views for and against it being taught.

Source 3

Domestic violence lessons: what do you think?

The following points of view have been offered on whether students should learn about the effects of domestic violence.

FOR

- The effects of domestic violence can leave children needing counselling – if they witness it then some may grow up assuming that violence is normal in relationships. Education about it should definitely happen.
- Schools should prepare young people for the real world – and domestic violence (and other issues) is a negative but real part of the world. School might be the place where young people can learn about helping agencies.
- Parents don't always find it easy to talk to children about social problems such as domestic violence – they may not know what to say. School can provide a clear message that all sorts of domestic violence is unacceptable.
- By having lessons in school a range of wider issues can also be raised; for example, many people believe that domestic violence is only committed by males on their partners and children – women too can be abusers, but this isn't often talked about.

AGAINST

- Lessons about domestic violence could make young people who are in such situations feel self-conscious that this had happened to them. Would they really be able to ask for and seek support if they felt this?
- Should there really be special lessons, as good teachers will already be introducing social topics into their classrooms? They should be able to judge when and how to do this rather than be told they have to and what to teach.
- Would lessons about domestic violence lead some children to be confused? At what age would they be able to distinguish between two people being verbally violent or simply having a row?
- You can't stop any problem by teaching about it. What will really help is spending time and effort on helping individuals who do suffer it to speak out and move on – school isn't the place for that.

ACTIVITY

Expect respect

2. Read about problems in teenage relationships in Source 2. Now turn this on its head and answer this question: In a teenage relationship, what things would show the couple respected each other?

ACTIVITY

PSHE topics

3. Read Source 3.
   a) What reasons would you add for or against lessons about domestic violence in PSHE?
   b) What are your views?

4. Whenever something is a social problem someone usually suggests there should be lessons about it in school – and that often means in PSHE. Do you think PSHE lessons are the place to put the world to rights? Offer arguments for and against.

5. What topic would you:
   a) add to PSHE
   b) remove from PSHE?

Where to turn for help and support

In this topic you will learn about:

- exploitation in relationships
- agencies that offer help and support.

You will explore:

- ways of recognising harm and risk in relationships
- ways to present information about helping agencies.

ACTIVITY

Who's out there?

1. Apart from the regular emergency services of police, ambulance and fire brigade, what other helping agencies do you know of?

In the previous topic you explored some of the ills that modern society experiences and looked at significant problems associated with grooming and domestic violence. By learning more about the agencies available to help, we can understand more. Perhaps in the future we may even find we are a 'signpost' to these agencies for friends, neighbours or acquaintances that are experiencing problems.

Source 1

Sharon and Paul

Sharon and Paul are 16 and have been seeing each other for a few months. They've been getting along really well until Paul started putting on the pressure. In front of their friends and family Paul is really charming – but when he and Sharon are alone it's a different story: He wants to have sex even when Sharon doesn't. He says things like 'If you don't do what I want I'm going to tell everyone that you're frigid.' or 'How will you feel when I put it round school that you're a lez?'. As well as using threatening language his behaviour is now beginning to show that he could be physically violent.

Support for Sharon
www.thesurvivorstrust.org

Source 2

Ebu and Grace

Grace has really enjoyed going out with Ebu – that is until last weekend when his behaviour suddenly changed. They were out together and Grace remembered that she'd promised to text her best friend. She started to do this and Ebu grabbed her wrist and said: 'What do you think you're doing – I didn't say you could do that.' It turns out he thinks he can and should control who Grace speaks to. His tone was so menacing that Grace was frightened of responding.

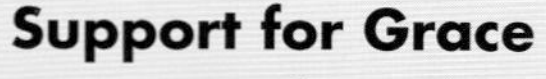

Support for Grace
www.youth2youth.co.uk – Run by young people for young people

Source 3

Simon

Simon is constantly abused by his partner: the abuse varies from aggressive comments and emotional bullying to hitting, kicking and slapping. Simon's partner also takes pleasure in belittling him in front of their friends and acquaintances.

Simon feels embarrassed because although he's heard about 'domestic violence' he thought it only happened to women. This means he feels he can't talk about it.

Support for Simon
www.mensadviceline.org.uk

Source 4

Jamila

22-year-old Jamila has learned that her parents are planning to make her travel to Pakistan. They want her to marry a man they had betrothed her to several years ago. This was done without her knowledge; she's never met the man she's meant to be matched with. She had been put into the engagement against her wishes. Her parents had gone quiet about this and she'd hoped they had listened to her opinions but quite recently the subject has been raised again. It is still not what she wants.

Support for Jamila
www.fco.gov.uk/en/travel-and-living-abroad/when-things-go-wrong/forced-marriage

Source 5

Irina

When she was seven Irina's mum married again. At first she got on well with her new stepfather but then he began to shout all the time and scare her. He occasionally slapped her mum and before long he was hitting Irina too. She had a lot of problems with school while this was going on and was often covered in bruises from her stepfather. She was embarrassed about what was happening at home and felt she couldn't talk to anyone about it.

Later on Irina found a boyfriend but after a while he became very controlling about what she wore, who she spoke to and who she was friends with. Because she had seen this happening to her mum, she thought it was normal, but when she asked her friends if this had happened to them they said it hadn't.

Support for Irina
www.thehideout.org.uk

Who can they speak to? — ACTIVITY

2. Read Sources 1–5. Each of the five people needs help and support. Choose one and research the helping agency listed for them. Plan a presentation about the agency. The presentation should include the following:

- name of the agency
- who it's run by and for
- how it can be accessed
- example(s) of how they've helped others.

Make your presentation as practical and helpful as possible. Include (if there are any) drawbacks or restrictions to using the agency in question. Your overall aim is that other students will be able to take away:

- an awareness of exploitation in relationships
- an ability to recognise harm in risky situations and know where to turn for help and support.

New to me — ACTIVITY

3. Which agency/agencies didn't you know about until today?

5 Diversity

Shared identity – shared experiences

In this topic you will learn about:
- factors that can unite people who come from different backgrounds
- examples of community service and citizenship schemes.

You will explore:
- ideas of what it means to be British
- how shared experiences might bring people together in positive ways.

Source 1 Being human

Maya Angelou is a black, female, American writer - but her thoughts, feelings, joys and sadness are understood and appreciated by all sorts of people across the world. She says: 'I speak to the *black* experience, but I am always talking about the human condition - about what we can endure, dream, fail at, and still survive.'

ACTIVITY

Being human

1. Imagine the quote in Source 1 with the word '*black*' replaced by any one of a series of words: *disabled, Jewish, old person*, etc. Does the shared experience of being human outweigh all the differences that can separate us?

Shared experiences unite us far more than our differences divide us. We all want good things for us and those we care about, we all face problems and need to overcome them, we all want to live in a world where we get fair treatment. Although people in Britain come from different backgrounds and cultures, we share much in common.

A survey in 2010, conducted by London Metropolitan University and Sheffield Hallam University, asked people who were training to teach history and citizenship what they thought of as characteristics of being British. Some of the British characteristics they mentioned are shown in Source 2.

Source 2 What is British?

Tolerance	Respect	Fair play	Politeness
Stoicism	Work ethic	Island mentality	Democracy
Queuing	Meritocracy	Snobbery	Rule of law
Being reserved	Christian morality	Xenophobia	Sense of humour

ACTIVITY

What is British?

2. Read Source 2 and discuss/answer the following questions:
   a) Which seem good characteristics of being British?
   b) Which seem negative?
   c) Do you think of these words when you think of 'Britishness'?
   d) What else would you add to the list?

One characteristic that people often think of as 'British' is a sense of community spirit and people helping each other out in difficult situations. Source 3 describes the idea of Britain having a national youth service scheme. One advantage of this scheme is that it would bring together young people who come from many different communities and backgrounds. The scheme would give them the experience of working together towards shared goals.

Source 3

The Cameron Plan for Teenagers

A pilot scheme has been set up by the Prime Minister which will provide a national service scheme for teenagers. This is part of his 'Big Society' idea – where different communities help and support each other.

Mr Cameron said the scheme would encourage people from different social backgrounds to mix, and would help address the 'tragic waste of potential in this country'.

Each young person who takes part will spend a minimum of 10 days and nights on activities which will include an outdoor adventure challenge and a set of structured tasks involving visiting and helping the local community. Communities will be asked what they feel they would most need help with.

'The young people of this country are as passionate and idealistic as any generation before – perhaps more passionate,' said the Prime Minister.

'But too many teenagers appear lost and feel their lives lack shape and direction. National Citizen Service will help change that. A kind of non-military national service, it's going to mix young people from different backgrounds in a way that doesn't happen right now.

'It's going to teach them what it means to be socially responsible. Above all, it's going to inspire a generation of young people to appreciate what they can achieve and how they can be part of the 'big society'.'

The first trial scheme involves 470 teenagers from London and Birmingham. The pilot schemes were welcomed by the Community Service Volunteers (CSV) – the leading volunteering charity in Britain.

Dame Elisabeth Hoodless, the executive director of CSV, said: '2010 is a historic turning point and a timely moment to look at nationwide community service in a fresh light. The crisis in care for frail elderly people who would prefer to remain in their own homes; the growing need for support for families under pressure; the alarming drop-out rates from higher education and the escalating rate of youth unemployment reinforces the benefits to our young people and to our communities of a year of full-time service for 18-year-olds. Finland, France, Germany, Israel and Italy have all taken the plunge. Why not here and now?'

National Youth Service

ACTIVITY

3. Read the article in Source 3 and discuss the following questions. Remember to give reasons to explain your point of view.

- **a)** Do you think the scheme would be popular amongst young people?
- **b)** What would be the advantages of bringing different types of people together through a shared experience?
- **c)** What are the positive things that young people might gain?
- **d)** Would this scheme provide a 'sense of belonging' for young people that discourages them from negative encounters; for example, gangs and gang violence?

Source 4 Celebrating new British Citizenship

Celebrating citizenship

ACTIVITY

4. Source 4 shows a photograph of new citizens celebrating. After taking part in the National Youth Service *all* young people could be offered a special recognition that they are now active citizens of their country. Draft some key words/ideas for the opening speech that the leader of the citizenship ceremony could make. The speech should outline what unites people and brings them together as citizens.

Challenging discrimination

In this topic you will learn about:
- the different forms that prejudice can take
- examples of people who have challenged discrimination.

You will explore:
- ways to build empathy and understanding
- how to take the initiative in challenging and combating discrimination and prejudice.

ACTIVITY

What can people do?

1. 'Rosa sat so Martin could walk so Barack could run.' Who are these people and what do you think this quotation means?

This chapter is about diversity and appreciating the similarities and differences between human beings. Sometimes people discriminate (intentionally and unintentionally) against things or people that they find strange, or do not understand. This topic addresses three different types of **discrimination** and uses examples for each:

- **prejudice** – attitudes towards refugees and asylum seekers
- **ignorance** – not knowing enough about and being afraid of HIV
- **thoughtlessness** – overlooking or not considering the needs of people with disabilities.

In each case you will be encouraged to think about taking the initiative in challenging these and other forms of discrimination.

Prejudice

The first source and activity looks at **refugees** and **asylum seekers**. It provides a window through which to look at some of the difficult decisions they have to make through necessity rather than choice.

Refugees leaving Banda Aceh, Indonesia

Colnbrook immigration removal centre near Heathrow airport is a short-term holding facility used to hold people immediately after their detention by the UK Immigration Service.

Source 1 Refugees and asylum seekers

A refugee is an exile who flees from their own country for safety. This may be as a result of war, natural disaster or being persecuted for reasons such as their race, religion, nationality, membership of a particular social group or political opinion.

An asylum seeker is a person who applies for protection and the right of residence in a foreign country.

The number of people forcibly uprooted by conflict and persecution worldwide stood at 42 million in 2008. The total includes 16 million refugees and asylum seekers and 26 million internally displaced people uprooted within their own countries.

About 80 per cent of the world's refugees live in developing countries, often in camps. Africa and Asia between them host more than three quarters of the world's refugees. Europe looks after just 14 per cent.

The UK is home to less than 2 per cent of the world's refugees – out of 16 million worldwide.

UNHCR (The United Nations Refugee Agency)

Having to leave ACTIVITY

2. Read Source 1. Refugees and asylum seekers generally receive very little empathy and understanding over their situation. This activity is about exploring how people feel when they are forced to make difficult decisions to become a stranger in a new country – and not by choice.

a) When you get home there is a note on the kitchen table saying you must leave in half an hour. You do not know where you are going or how long for, or if you will ever see your home again. You can only take a small rucksack. List the 10 items that you want to take with you.

b) Also on the kitchen table are three tickets. These have been incredibly difficult to obtain because they are rationed. Decide which two people out of all your family and friends will come with you.

Ignorance

Source 2 and the activity 'Children with HIV' move on to looking at discrimination caused by ignorance. People often 'fear' something because they don't truly understand it and then they make judgements before knowing the true facts.

Source 2

Schools close doors on HIV charity's kids camp

A series of schools have refused to let a leading children's HIV charity use their facilities for a summer camp, raising fears of widespread discrimination. The Children's HIV Association (CHIVA) made bookings with the schools. These were later cancelled after it became known that the young people attending would be HIV-positive.

The camp, for 100 young people aged 13 to 17, plus 60 volunteers, was scheduled to take place when the schools' own pupils would have been away. But the charity, an association of health experts, struggled to find a school that would hire out its facilities.

One head told CHIVA he would not allow his school to be used because parents would not like it. Another agreed to the booking but cancelled after being told of the children's HIV status.

The school said it had realised it could not offer CHIVA the accommodation it needed. But the charity obtained a number of emails between senior school staff entitled 'health matters'. This suggests the real reason for the offer being withdrawn was not about accommodation.

And a third school said it could not comply with the charity's request for confidentiality. The charity had asked that only a couple of key senior staff be informed of who was hiring the school in order to protect the identity of the young people attending.

Paddy McMaster, chair of CHIVA and consultant paediatrician at the University Hospital of North Staffordshire, said: 'Generally, there is discrimination and a lot of misunderstanding about HIV in schools. With the summer camp, it's not possible to prove discrimination but that is the most likely explanation given the sequence of events and the responses we got. What can be perceived by some schools as a justifiable reason for not wanting to include children with HIV is, in fact, discrimination.'

Dr McMaster said children with HIV are encouraged not to discuss their infection with their peers because of the stigma still attached to it. 'This year is the first in which the charity has organised a summer camp. It allows them to be in a community where they can talk freely and see they are not alone,' he said.

The camp, which is funded by the Elton John Aids Foundation (EJAF), is now due to go ahead in another school. It will include sessions on rights, sexual health and medication.

Anne Aslett, executive director of EJAF, said: 'It's horrifying to think that school trustees, teachers and even parents in this country might still be so misinformed about HIV/AIDS that HIV-positive children could be stigmatised and discriminated against.'

TES, 21 May 2010

Children with HIV

3. Read Source 2 and discuss the following questions:
   - **a)** Do you understand how HIV is transmitted? In the light of factual information about HIV did the schools have anything to worry about?
   - **b)** What do you think your school would say if it was asked to provide facilities for a CHIVA summer camp?
   - **c)** Look at your school's equal opportunities policy to find out if discrimination against people with HIV is covered.
   - **d)** Are there other school policies that ensure people with HIV won't suffer from discrimination?

Thoughtlessness

The final source and activity look at how people with disabilities are viewed, treated and often represented by others. It uses a media example of this prejudicial and thoughtless discrimination.

Source 3 Prejudicial attitudes

In 2009 the BBC employed presenter Cerrie Burnell to work on their children's channel, CBeebies. Cerrie was born with only one hand and when she appeared on television the press revealed that complaints were sparked from parents who claimed that the CBeebies host was frightening their children.

There were reports that some parents said they would prefer it if their children did not see or hear about people with disabilities.

A father explained that he didn't want his children watching because he felt it would have played on his daughter's mind and possibly caused her sleep problems.

Other parents felt that it was forcing them to discuss disability before their children were ready.

However, there were also those who expressed their support for the presenter and the BBC, voicing that if a child asks questions then they are old enough to understand the answer.

Some parents felt children simply accept the world as presented to them and did not have problems in accepting people with disabilities. A few revealed they were delighted to have been given the opportunity to talk about people's differences and everyone being individual. One person verbalised the rich diversity of the world we live in, explaining that if parents are so negative about encountering people who are different from them (whether it be religion, skin colour, height, weight, disability, etc.) their child will be growing up with a distorted view of reality.

A handful went on to applaud the BBC for employing someone for their ability to do the job, irrespective of any disability.

Speaking for herself, Cerrie said, 'That this has happened at all is really just a sign that we need to have more disabled people on telly.'

Point of view

4. Read Source 3.
   - **a)** What do you think of the different attitudes expressed in it?
   - **b)** How do you feel about the fact that most of the people we see on TV are able-bodied, attractive, slender, under 45 years old, etc?
   - **c)** Write a letter to the BBC explaining your point of view and expressing your opinions as a future television licence payer.

ACTIVITY

Combating prejudice

5. 'It is harder to crack a prejudice than an atom.' (Albert Einstein)
   What is it about prejudice that makes it so difficult to combat?

Discrimination through invisibility

In this topic you will learn about:

- the prejudice of invisibility
- how and where LGB people are portrayed on TV.

You will explore:

- an example of how prejudicial language can cause harm
- how people from minority groups are portrayed on TV.

ACTIVITY

Who can you name?

1. Can you name five national or international figures who are LGB?
2. Does it make a difference to how we think of a public figure if they reveal that they are LGB?

Invisibility

The previous topic looked at examples of discrimination and how they could be challenged. It is easier to challenge prejudices when we are aware of them. However, one form of prejudice not so easily tackled is that of 'invisibility'. In other words, not including any representation of people who may be different.

It may be that people of some ethnicities, religions, cultures, abilities or disabilities, genders, ages or sexual orientations are omitted from news reports, TV programmes, films, novels, adverts, etc. – and, as a result, become 'invisible' in the media.

For example, although black people had been involved in the media for twenty years before, it wasn't until 1990 that Blue Peter hired somebody who wasn't white – Diane-Louise Jordan joined as one of their presenters in January that year.

One group of people who have often continued to be invisible are **LGB** people – that is those who identify themselves as lesbian, gay or bisexual. The prejudice of invisibility is explored by using some examples associated with LGB issues.

Unseen on TV

3. Read Source 1 and discuss and answer the following questions:
   a) Do the results of the survey surprise you? Why?
   b) Looking back over the last few months, can you identify a positive and negative example of LGB people/characters on TV?
   c) LGB people are not the only group that can end up being invisible:
   - Do a short comparison survey looking at these examples: people with a physical disability and/ or a learning disability; fat people; senior citizens; people with mental health problems.
   - In which programmes have you seen them and how were they portrayed?

Source 1

Unseen on screen

Groundbreaking research published by Stonewall has found that ordinary gay people are almost invisible on the 20 TV programmes most watched by Britain's young people.

Young people from across Britain interviewed by researchers said that gay people on TV are largely stereotyped as leading unhappy lives and bullied and rejected by their families. They also said they rely on TV to learn about gay people.

Researchers monitored 20 TV programmes most popular with young people on BBC1, BBC2, ITV1, Channel 4 and 5 for a 16-week period. This revealed that ordinary lesbian, gay and bisexual people are practically invisible.

Just 46 minutes out of 126 hours of output showed gay people positively and realistically. Almost half of all portrayal was stereotypical, with gay people being depicted as figures of fun, predatory, promiscuous or tragic.

- 39 per cent of portrayal was in soap operas and 33 per cent was in reality TV.
- There was negligible reflection of gay people in magazine shows and talent shows and no portrayal in drama programmes.
- There were 39 minutes that made passing reference to gay people – half of these references depicted gay people largely for comic effect.
- Almost 20 per cent of references used being gay, or the possibility of being gay, to tease or insult.
- 17 minutes of programming depicted homophobia but 59 per cent of this went unchallenged. Just seven minutes featured scenes where homophobia was challenged.
- 17 and 18-year-old young gay people simply don't relate to gay people they see on TV.
- Young people want to see positive and realistic portrayal of LGB people on TV and think it would have a positive effect on their own attitudes and behaviour and that of their peers.

Source 2

What Do We Do with a Variation?
by James Berry

What do we do with a difference?
Do we stand and discuss its oddity
or do we ignore it?

Do we shut our eyes to it
or poke it with a stick?
Do we clobber it to death?

Do we move around it in rage
and enlist the rage of others?
Do we will it to go away?

Do we look at it in awe
or purely in wonderment?
Do we work for it to disappear?

Do we pass it stealthily
or change route away from it?
Do we will it to become like ourselves?

What do we do with a difference?
Do we communicate to it,
let application acknowledge it
for barriers to fall down?

When I Dance (Peters, Fraser and Dunlop Group Ltd/ Harcourt Brace, 1988)

What Do We Do with a Variation?

4. Read Source 2. What do you think is the message of this poem?

6 Values

Individual, family and community values

In this topic you will learn about:
- different values
- ways of describing society.

You will explore:
- your own and other people's values
- the effect of different or conflicting values.

ACTIVITY

What do you take with you?

1. When people are faced with a crisis (e.g. fire, flood, etc.) and have to flee their home, they can only take what they can carry. Assuming you'd take your money, jewellery, laptop and pets, what else would you take?

ACTIVITY

Me and my values

2. How would you answer the following questions for yourself:
   - What do I value?
   - Why do I value it?
   - Where have our values developed from?

   Be honest. Remember for the purposes of this activity that your values will not be marked or judged and it is OK to think and act differently from others.

Values

In the first activity you may have decided to take with you objects that have value to you alone and that are irreplaceable because of the meaning they have to you. The special meaning they have for you will be affected by the values you hold.

Values can be defined as:
- Qualities
- Principles
- Standards

... of what is important in life.

(*Oxford English Dictionary*)

Your personal experiences and your life experiences are different from those of the people around you – everyone is an individual.

Your personal values are:
- your own
- individual
- distinctive
- instinctive?
- learned?

Each of us will have individual values, often shaped by our families, our upbringing and where we go to school. There are also overarching 'big' values that often reflect the culture, laws and traditions of a society. These values are shared values. Some are shown in Source 1.

Source 1 Twelve values

ACTIVITY

Explaining our values

3. We often take the 'big' values listed in Source 1 for granted, and don't make time to talk about what they mean for us. What personal meaning do they hold for you?

a) Decide which:
- has some importance
- is important
- is very important
- is the most important.

b) Now rank them in order of importance for you.

Differences between people are often largely based on a range of different beliefs and values. The importance people put on 'big' values will depend on a variety of factors including their culture, faith, etc. In a multi-cultural society such as ours people will approach different issues in different ways depending on the values they have. For example – what is our attitude towards care for elderly people? Some cultures and communities value their elders and see caring for them at home as an expression of love and respect for them. Others, whilst valuing the elderly, do not think that paying others to care for their elderly means they love and respect them less.

The next activity explores other situations that will be affected by the values people hold.

Source 2 'Issues'

Issue 1: Sadie is worried that the small child next door is being abused. She has not reported it.

Issue 2: Jake decides to cover for his mate Ben who has broken the law.

Issue 5: Mr Lehmann the banker accepts a huge monetary bonus at a time of financial crisis.

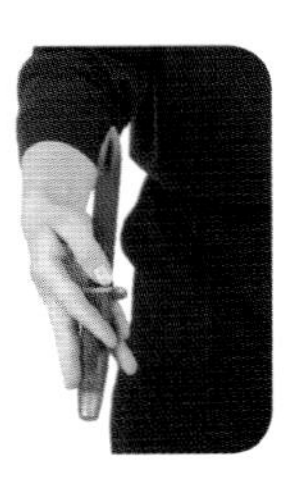

Issue 6: Freddie carries a weapon for protection.

ACTIVITY

Issues and values

4. In groups, choose two of the issues from Source 2.

a) Using the values listed in Source 1 decide which could be relevant to each of your two issues. The values you choose may come from different viewpoints. Give examples for each value chosen; for example, tolerance could be one of the values associated with issue 1 – Sadie might think families have the right to bring up children as they choose.

b) Discuss the values you have decided on for each issue:
- Which value do you think is the most important in terms of how the community should respond?
- Which value would most likely help everyone to reach a consensus?

c) Now answer the following questions:
- Was it easy to see the issue from more than one point of view?
- How tolerant are we of other people's views when they differ from our own?
- Were there two or three key values that trumped all the others?

Issue 3: Smithy thinks it's clever that he lives off benefits rather than working.

Issue 4: Cindy gets drunk and incapable on Saturday nights when she is in town.

Scenarios based on an activity from *Beliefs, Values and Attitudes* (Me-and-Us Ltd, 2009)

ACTIVITY

Affirmation

5. If your school yearbook celebrated you for one of the twelve values listed in Source 1, which would you hope it would be and why?

Diverse and conflicting values

In this topic you will learn about:

- different ways of making a decision
- examples of current issues on which people hold different values.

You will explore:

- strategies for making decisions
- responses to diverse and conflicting values.

Source 1 What do you value?

ACTIVITY

Values and actions

1. We live in a very busy society where adults seem to have less time to give to family life. What do you think of the values of the parent in Source 1?
2. What value or values do you hold that make you act in a certain way?

In Source 1 the parent made a conscious decision to do something in a particular way; that is, spend more time with their family. Values affect the decisions we make. How often do we stop and think before making a decision?

Source 2 Ways of making a decision

- **a) Acting on impulse (what I feel like doing there and then).**
- **b) Considering the consequences (what might happen).**
- **c) Considering the effect it will have on others.**
- **d) Doing what everyone else does.**
- **e) Doing what my friends say.**
- **f) Going along with what's easiest.**
- **g) Letting others decide for me.**
- **h) Talking it through with someone I trust.**
- **i) Trusting my feelings.**

ACTIVITY

Deciding how to act

3. Look at Source 2.
   - **a)** How important would each of these approaches be in helping you arrive at a decision? Prioritise the different ways by putting them into a diamond nine as below.

     1
     2 3
     4 5 6
     7 8
     9

   - **b)** Now discuss the following questions:
     - Which are the most thoughtful decision-making options?
     - Is it right to go along with others even if you don't support what they plan to do?
     - Should you let others make decisions for you?

ACTIVITY

Different values

4. Look at Sources 3–5. What do you think about these news stories? Use the nine statements in Source 2 as a base for coming to a conclusion about what you would do.

Source 3

New Zealand votes to give parents the right to smack children – UK parents want to do the same!

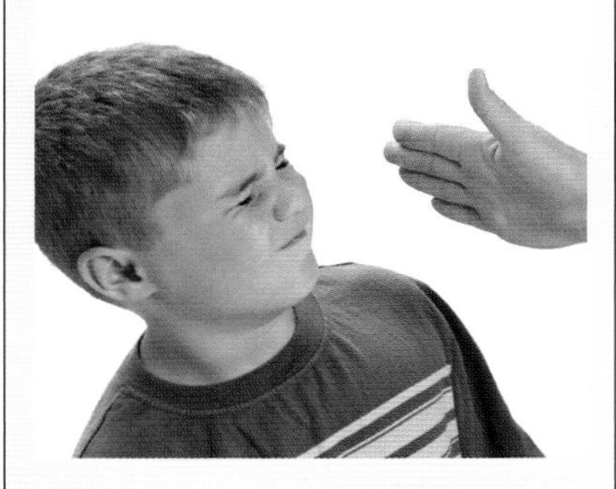

In 2009 New Zealanders overwhelmingly voted (by almost 90 per cent) to reinstate a parent's right to smack their children.

UK parents groups say that they want all restrictions on smacking children lifted too – so that any parent can punish their child as they see fit. At the moment UK law says it is unlawful for a parent or carer to smack their child, except where this amounts to 'reasonable punishment'.

On the other hand there is huge pressure from different organisations in the UK to change the law relating to reasonable punishment. Organisations such as the NSPCC campaign for a complete ban on all smacking of children by their parents.

Source 4

Half of the UK population backs death penalty

The latest poll shows 54 per cent of people back the death penalty while 30 per cent are against it. Many even believe the death penalty should be extended beyond murderers to rapists and drug traffickers.

Calls for the death penalty have been heightened by recent high-profile cases, including the torture and killing of Baby P in 2009.

But human rights activists say support for the death penalty is actually weakening and claim the moral case against the punishment remains strong. The last British executions were in 1964, before capital punishment was scrapped for murder in 1969 and for all offences in 1998.

The strongest support comes from older generations, but one person in three aged 16 to 24 also supports executions.

Outlawing capital punishment is a condition of European Union membership and a European Convention on Human Rights protocol, which Britain signed in 1999. Human rights charity Reprieve last night insisted: 'In our experience, the British people have a sane and humane attitude towards the death penalty and would never tolerate executions on our soil.'

Source 5

French ban on religious symbols comes into force

A law banning Islamic headscarves and other religious symbols from French state schools has come into effect. So far, most pupils have been observing the law by removing the headscarf or other symbols before entering school.

The law affects 12 million children. The ban is designed to maintain France's tradition of strictly separating state and religion. It forbids state school students from wearing 'conspicuous' religious apparel. Jewish skullcaps, Sikh turbans and large Christian crosses are also banned.

In the UK some commentators want the same ban applied in schools so that religious symbols can only be worn in faith-based schools.

Core values

5. Is there a particular value that you would hold to, whatever the changing circumstances in your life?

7 Consumerism

Responsible consumerism

In this topic you will learn about:

- advertising techniques that encourage spending
- food wastage in the UK.

You will explore:

- the real value of retail 'offers'
- actions that retailers can take towards responsible food use.

All sorts of things affect our choices as consumers (for example, cost; taste and appearance; brand loyalty; ethical concerns such as food miles, fairtrade, animal testing, impact on environment, etc.). In this topic you are going to look at what it means to be a responsible consumer, and in particular you are going to look at how the following might influence our choices:

- price/special offers as a factor in influencing choice
- concerns around how supermarkets deal with waste.

ACTIVITY

Special offers?

1. Look at the photos and information in Source 1. What special offers are shown and described? Can you think of any others?
2. **a)** Have you ever:
   - bought an item of clothing from a 'sale' and then not worn it
   - thrown away food from a two-for-one offer because it went off before it could be used
   - ended up realising it wasn't such a 'good deal' after all the extras were added?

   b) Do you think you have ever been 'taken in' by any of these?

Source 1 Special offers?

The responsible consumer can spot the real bargain ...

Shops are full of special offers, but some of them aren't that special, and even break government guidelines.

Organisations such as 'Which?' and the Office of Fair Trading (OFT) investigated offers at high street and online retailers to check if they complied with government guidelines to ensure that offers don't mislead customers.

- Some pricing tactics encourage spending unnecessarily, with complex pricing including '2 for 1' and 'Buy One Get One Free' (BOGOF) offers. Three in 10 consumers said that BOGOF offers resulted in them throwing away unused food.
- Some gig and concert promoters use 'drip pricing', where the cost of an item grows through the buying process; extra charges – for example, taxes, credit card fees or delivery – are levelled only when a buyer is part way through the process.
- Some retailers use 'baiting' techniques; for example, clothing shops using banner headlines saying 'Half Price Sale', when only some items are available at discounted prices.

Money Matters, Office of Fair Trading and Which?

One way of defining a responsible consumer is somebody who understands but is not taken in by the power of persuasive advertising. They are able to be socially responsible and selective over what they purchase.

Responsible consumerism

3. We would all like to think of ourselves as responsible consumers but inevitably most of us get drawn into buying things. One way to look at our own spending habits is to think of our 'Wants versus Needs'.
   a) Make a list of everything you can remember buying (or that was bought for you) in the last six months. Categorise them into 'wants' or 'needs'.
   b) Work with another person to compare your lists. Did you find they had the same views on what constituted 'needs'?
4. How easy is it to be socially responsible and selective in the face of sophisticated and persuasive advertising?

Food wastage

The Waste & Resources Action Programme (WRAP) in 2010 found that there was significant food wastage across the UK; for example:

- The average UK household needlessly throws away 18 per cent of all food purchased. Families with children throw away 27 per cent.
- £1 billion worth of food wasted in the UK was still 'in date'.
- Meat and fish made up a large proportion of the total waste. For example, 5500 whole chickens were thrown away each day.
- 'Mixed foods' like ready meals made up 21 per cent of the total cost of waste, with 440,000 thrown away each day.
- Yoghurt was a commonly abandoned product, with an estimated 1.3 million unopened pots disposed of each day.

Why do people buy more food than they can use? Supermarkets need to provide more information so that responsible consumers can make informed choices. Consumers need to let supermarkets know what change is needed.

Source 2
8.3 million tonnes of food is thrown away by households in the UK every year, having a damaging effect on the environment.

Source 3 Food – some ways to reduce waste

Late-night sandwich run

Chris has been homeless for eight years. In and out of hostels, he is now sleeping rough. He is offered a sandwich (donated by Pret A Manger) by Mark, a volunteer from the Simon Community, a registered charity providing aid to homeless people throughout central London.

Each year Pret A Manger donates 1.7 million products across the UK, and 96 per cent of their shops give unsold food to homeless charities every day.

The influential watchdog the Sustainable Development Commission (SDC) estimated shops were throwing away 1.6 million tonnes of food a year, so any waste-saving schemes are welcome. More and more shops are thinking inventively about waste and distributing leftovers to those in need.

What other shops are doing

- **Tesco:** Any waste is either re-used, recycled or turned into energy, and they divert all their waste from landfill. They work with charity FareShare, who distribute fit-to-eat unsold food to those in need.
- **Waitrose:** Very small amount of food left over, but work with FareShare in same way as Tesco. 115 branches generate renewable energy from waste.
- **Co-op:** Supports WRAP's 'Love Food Hate Waste' campaign, which aims to raise awareness of the need to reduce food waste.
- **Sainsbury's:** Minimises food waste through accurate forecasting and stock control. Donates to FareShare, and food that can't be eaten is used to generate electricity through processes such as anaerobic digestion.

The benefits are not just environmental; there are commercial considerations too, as the 'low-waste' message is something that is important to more and more customers. More information can be found at:

- WRAP: household food waste (www.wrap.org.uk)
- Love Food Hate Waste campaign (www.lovefoodhatewaste.com)
- FareShare: community food network (www.fareshare.org.uk).

ACTIVITY

Responsible food use

5. Some supermarkets are already working towards using leftover food to help those in need (see opposite). Research the policies about not throwing out useable food of other supermarket chains that are not mentioned.

ACTIVITY

One personal step

6. Responsible consumerism needs each individual to make changes. What one personal step could you take to ensure you become a more responsible consumer?

Ethical consumerism

In this topic you will learn about:

- what can make consumerism unethical
- the human cost of manufacturing in developing countries.

You will explore:

- ethical and unethical factors in goods production
- different attitudes towards the concept of 'fair pricing'.

Ethical consumerism means ensuring that the products we buy do not impact negatively on people and the environment. The following are ethical concerns:

- working conditions for staff (including not exploiting child labour)
- fair pay
- environmental sustainability of materials used; for example, recyclable, energy efficient
- animal welfare issues
- ethical profit sharing; for example, Fairtrade
- ethical investment policy; for example, not working with arms dealers.

A major ethical concern is where in the world goods are made and whether anyone has been exploited to make them. Cheap clothing for western markets is often manufactured by multinational companies in **developing** or **newly industrialised countries** because:

- wages and other overheads are lower
- capital spending (for example, building a factory) is cheaper
- employment laws are less strict (for example, around children working)
- raw materials are cheaper.

This creates new employment opportunities and income for poor families and export income for the country, but sometimes working conditions are exploitative.

ACTIVITY

Ethical consumerism

1. What does 'ethical consumerism' mean to you?

ACTIVITY

Is low price always fair price?

2. Look at the labels of the shirt/blouse, trousers/skirt, shoes/sandals that you are wearing. Where were they made? Chances are they were made in a developing or newly industrialised country such as China, Sri Lanka, Bangladesh or India.
3. One way to produce low-price goods is to produce them in situations where the workers do not have employment rights and where wages are low (see Source 1). What do you think the five people listed in Source 1 say in response to this question:

   Do consumers need to pay fairer prices (which sometimes may be more than they pay now) to ensure goods are ethically produced?

ACTIVITY

What else do you want to know?

4. Read Source 2, which gives examples of the sorts of questions ethical consumers have asked in the past. What questions would you like to see answered to help you become a more ethical consumer?

Source 1 People concerned about clothing production

The textile, clothing and footwear industry is labour-intensive and factories in developing countries are sometimes associated with the term 'sweatshop', where workers can be treated poorly, with low wages, long hours and poor safety conditions. Fairtrade campaigns have led to codes of conduct and goods being certified, but also to the closure of factories, which can worsen the situation of poor people.

People concerned about clothing production include:

1. Clothing factory worker in a developing country

In some countries farmers have suffered great hardship and been attracted by the possibilities of working in new factories opening up in the towns. It means separation from their families, but often accommodation is provided and regular wages help them assist their family by sending money home. The conditions may not be regulated.

2. Chief Executive Officer (CEO) of a multinational clothing company

Shareholders want improved profits and so manufacturing off shore with cheaper labour and attractive tax deals is an appealing option.

3. Environmentalist

The production and manufacture of textiles and clothing and footwear have high environmental demands, such as water and energy, waste disposal and pollution.

4. Non-Governmental Organisation (NGO) worker

Tight manufacturing deadlines and costs mean unskilled people can be at risk of exploitation. Local **NGO**s work with vulnerable people to empower them to protect their rights. They also work with governments, businesses and other NGOs to assist in creating better working conditions for factory workers in developing countries.

5. Ethical consumer

Many people feel concerned about the economic, environmental and social problems resulting from some practices in the textile, clothing and footwear manufacturing industry and want to do something about it, such as carefully choosing what they do and don't buy.

Source 2

You ask … they answer

When it comes to being an ethical consumer it is sometimes difficult to debunk the myth from the reality. Expert advice is often offered to consumers through newspapers and specialist websites. Some common questions and answers are:

Q1: Do some companies only supply green (renewable) energy?
There are very few companies that supply renewable energy alone. One example of these is Good Energy, who supply only renewable electricity to homes and businesses.

Q2: Is it more environmentally friendly to buy paper that has been recycled, such as toilet paper or paper for the printer?
Between 28 and 70 per cent less energy is used to produce recycled paper. It also uses less water. For example, recycled toilet paper uses 50 per cent less energy than creating virgin toilet paper; this means it is a better option if you want to reduce your carbon impact. The same applies to A4 paper, though the quality isn't as good if you need high-quality printing.

Q3: Which bank is best for ethical policies?
The Co-op Bank was a pioneer for ethical bank accounts and is still the only ethical high street bank, although there are other banks such as Triodos Bank and Charity Bank. Co-op Insurance is one of two top-performing insurers ethically.

Consumerism and giving

In this topic you will learn about:

- charities and the methods they use to raise funds
- charitable giving and ethical banking.

You will explore:

- your personal attitudes towards charitable giving
- ethical values that affect investments.

Over half of all adults in the UK donated to charitable causes in 2008/09. The National Council for Voluntary Organisations estimated that the total amount given may be as much as £9.9 billion.

Charities raise funds through some of the following methods:

- tin shakers; for example, outside supermarkets
- door-to-door collections; for example, envelope returns
- street fundraisers; for example, people who stop you on the street and get you to sign up
- events to raise funds; for example, sponsored runs/coffee mornings
- charity shops; for example, Oxfam/local hospice
- appeals; for example, website donations
- friends of ...; for example, people who regularly support and give.

Charities work in many different ways – two examples are:

- emergency aid – where they help people affected by natural disasters; for example, floods
- development work – where they help people to develop skills to improve their situation.

What would you do?

1. You are walking through the town centre. Someone who looks homeless holds out a cup and asks you for some change. What do you do?

ACTIVITY

What's the priority for your money?

2. If you decided to donate to charity, would you give for emergency aid or development work? Start by thinking about what each can provide and then decide what your priority would be.

There are so many charities trying to raise funds it's not easy to work out which, if any, to give to. If a person does choose to give to charity, it may help them if they consider which charities make the most of their money before they make a final decision. For example:

✓ What percentage of the donation does the charity use for administration/costs?

✓ Does the charity maximise the amount it is given by providing 'givers' with a Gift Aid form, which increases the value of the donation? Gift Aid means that you make a tax agreement that allows the charity to claim more money back.

✓ How they give; for example, if they give via a website such as www.purecharity.org.uk or www.justgiving.com it is important to check whether a percentage of what is given is taken off for administration, as some charity donation websites take a large percentage from the donor before it gets to the charity.

Ethical banking

An ethical bank is one that is concerned with social and environmental issues and also how its investments and loans impact on others.

Other names for such banks are social, alternative, civic or sustainable banks. An ethical bank will make sure their investments reflect their customers' views on issues that are important to them. Many people don't give much thought to how their money will be used by banks and other investment companies. However, some people choose an ethical option for their personal banking.

When surveyed, customers of ethical banks expressed concerns about:

- animal welfare
- child labour
- climate change
- ecological impact
- fair trade
- human rights
- international development.

ACTIVITY

Ways to donate

3. Find out more about ways that people can give to charity.

ACTIVITY

How would you choose?

4. What important factors do you think people should consider before investing their money?

ACTIVITY

Who do I give to?

5. You've won £1000 to divide equally between one national/local charity and one international charity. Which charities would you choose and why?

8 Personal Finance

Budgeting

In this topic you will learn about:

- tax: how and why we pay it
- budgeting for a new home
- planning for a secure financial future.

You will explore:

- different tax rates and the services that taxes provide
- the cost of living when moving into a new home – needs and wants
- current and savings accounts and pension schemes.

Most people would like to have more money; the amount of money you earn has a direct impact on your lifestyle. Having 'lots of money' means that you can do the things you really want to do or buy the things you really want to buy. Having 'just enough' money could mean that you only just 'get by' and have to be careful what you spend your money on. You are more likely to spend it on things you need as opposed to things you want.

Most people earn money by working. The money you get paid for working is your wages and you receive a pay slip to show how much you have earned. When you get your pay slip you will see two different payments, as shown in Source 1.

Source 1 A pay slip

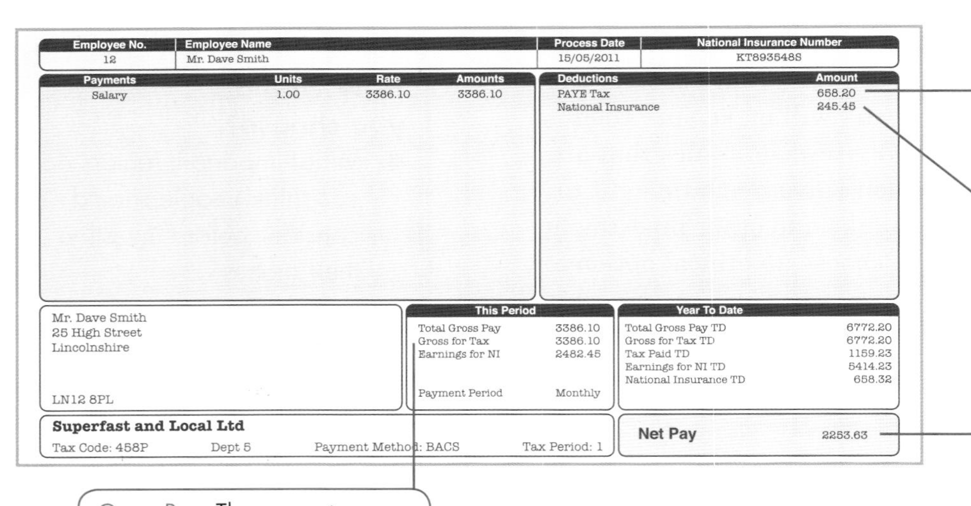

Employee No.	Employee Name	Process Date	National Insurance Number
12	Mr. Dave Smith	15/05/2011	KT893548S

Payments	Units	Rate	Amounts
Salary	1.00	3386.10	3386.10

Deductions	Amount
PAYE Tax	658.20
National Insurance	245.45

Mr. Dave Smith
25 High Street
Lincolnshire

LN12 8PL

This Period	
Total Gross Pay	3386.10
Gross for Tax	3386.10
Earnings for NI	2482.45
Payment Period	Monthly

Year To Date	
Total Gross Pay TD	6772.20
Gross for Tax TD	6772.20
Tax Paid TD	1159.23
Earnings for NI TD	5414.23
National Insurance TD	658.32

Superfast and Local Ltd
Tax Code: 458P Dept 5 Payment Method: BACS Tax Period: 1

Net Pay 2253.63

PAYE Tax: Money taken by the government to provide a wide range of services that we need in society, such as education, health, transport, emergency services and defence.

National Insurance: National Insurance contributions are paid to fund state pensions, unemployment benefits and sickness and disability allowance.

Net Pay: The amount you actually receive.

Gross Pay: The amount you earn before any deductions are made for tax or pension contributions.

Tax rates

In 2011/12 everyone could earn up to £7475 before they had to start paying tax. Once you earn more you pay tax at the rates shown in Source 2.

Source 2 Tax rates in 2011–12

Amount earned	% of earning paid in tax
£0–£7475	0
£6475–£35,000	20 (basic tax rate)
£35,001–£150,000)	40 (higher tax rate)
Over £150,000	50 (additional rate)

You can also be charged tax on the following: earnings from self-employment; most pensions' income; interest on most savings; income from shares (dividends); rental income; income paid to you from a trust.

ACTIVITY

Why do we need to pay tax?

1. What would happen to society if we didn't pay tax? Discuss all the problems we would face; for example, those who couldn't afford to pay for their own healthcare would have to go without treatment.
2. Look at Source 2. Do you think it is fair that different people pay different tax rates depending on how much they earn? Explain your answer.

Mortgages

Unless you have an endless supply of money you will need to budget your income carefully, particularly if you want to buy your own home in the future.

The two main ways to repay your mortgage are 'repayment' and 'interest only'. With a repayment mortgage you make monthly repayments for an agreed period (usually 25 years) until you've paid back the loan and the interest. The interest rate will vary depending on the type of mortgage you choose.

With an interest-only mortgage you make monthly repayments for an agreed period but these will only cover the interest on your loan (endowment mortgages work in this way). You'll normally also have to pay into another savings or investment plan that'll hopefully pay off the loan at the end of the term.

Depending on the type of repayments you are making you could end up paying back twice the amount you borrowed. Although this sounds very expensive, it does allow people to own their own property and have a secure investment, providing they have kept up with their repayments.

ACTIVITY

How well could I budget?

3. **a)** Make a list of the different things you would have to pay for on a monthly basis if you moved into a one-bedroom flat; for example, mortgage or rent, water rates, council tax, etc. Include essentials such as food, but also other things that you would like to have in your home.
   b) Try and put a monthly monetary value on each of the things on your list. Your teacher will be able to give you some ideas about costs or you could research them on the internet. When you have the monetary values, add them together to get a total.
   c) Go back through your list and highlight things that are essential in one colour and things that are desirable in another; for example, if you have included satellite or cable TV you need to think whether this is really necessary.
   d) Work out you new monthly expenditure based solely on the essential things. Now times this value by twelve (for each month of the year).

Savings

Remember that in addition to the essentials you need to spend your money on, you will also want to have money left to buy other things that you want.

The money you have left after paying for all your essentials is known as your **disposable income**. This is the money you may choose to buy new clothes, DVDs or games with, or go out for dinner, the cinema or whatever else you like to do. Another option, however, is to consider saving or investing some of your disposable income for the future.

You could save into your regular (current) bank account. This will mean that you can access the money as and when you need it by using you bank/debit card. However, if you intend to save some money on a regular basis there are other types of savings accounts that will earn you more interest. One example of this is through a type of account called an Individual Savings Account, often know as an ISA. ISAs are tax-free savings accounts, which means you do not have to pay tax on any interest earned.

To get the best deal on bank and savings accounts it is important to 'shop around' to see which offer you the best deals. Some will offer other incentives such as free overdrafts or mobile banking.

ACTIVITY

Which account should I choose?

4. a) Research and select one bank account you think would be most suitable for you to have your wages paid into each month and one savings account that would be best to save into. Some of the comparison websites such as www.moneysupermarket.com are particularly useful for researching this as they give you a quick overview of each account. You will need to find out the following things about each type of account:

Current account	Savings account
Which bank it is with	Which bank it is with
Cost of banking (often free)	Minimum monthly payments needed
Overdraft facility	Interest rates
Card provided (Visa, etc.)	How quickly you can access funds
Interest given on money in account	Other incentives
Overdraft facility & cost	
Amount needed to open account	
Other incentives	

Once you have selected the most appropriate account for you, write down the details.

b) In small groups, explain to each other why you have chosen your particular current and savings account:

- What were the advantages and disadvantages of each account?
- What was the most and the least important factor when deciding?

Pensions

Another way to save for your future is a pension. This is a source of income that people receive when they retire. You may have heard a great deal of talk about pensions over recent months. This is because the population as a whole is ageing and therefore more people need greater support financially, for longer. You may find that you will be expected to work to at least 70+ to receive your state pension, rather than retire at the current age of 60 for women and 65 for men. The pension age for men and women has already risen to 66 from the year 2020.

When planning your retirement there are three main types of pension you need to consider. These are:

- the state pension
- personal pensions
- company pensions.

State pension

The state pension is a regular payment people can claim when they get to state pension age. Most people build up some state pension, but the amount they get varies depending on how many years they have paid national insurance contributions – to get the full state pension you need to have contributed for 30 years.

Personal pensions

Personal pensions (also known as private pensions) provide you with a regular income in your retirement. It works by making regular payments during your working life, and the more you can afford to pay in, the more you will receive when you retire.

Company pensions

Company pensions are set up by employers to provide pensions for their employees on retirement. They are also sometimes called occupational or workplace pensions. Both the employer and employee contribute to this type of pension scheme.

ACTIVITY

The dream retirement

5. a) Describe the type of lifestyle you would like to have when you retire.

b) Consider all the things you will need to do as from now to achieve this, and make a plan. In your plan show the different stages of your life and what you will need to do at each stage to achieve your retirement lifestyle. You could include the stages 16, 18, 24, 40, 50, 60 and 70+. You will need to include details about education, career choices, mortgages, savings and lifestyles.

ACTIVITY

Planning for my own future

6. How important do you think it is to plan for your financial future?

Credit and debt

In this topic you will learn about:

- financial risks associated with credit and debt
- how credit providers make money through interest payments
- advantages and disadvantages of credit and store cards.

You will explore:

- how the use of credit cards can lead to a 'debt trap'
- how debt can lead to bankruptcy and insolvency
- the different types of credit cards that are available.

You will no doubt have heard of terms such as 'debt' and 'credit'. But what do they actually mean and how are they linked?

Understanding debt and credit

1. a) In pairs, discuss what you think the terms debt and credit mean. Give examples to show your understanding.

b) Where have you heard these terms? Do you hear them frequently?

c) Do you associate them with being positive or negative?

Most people within the UK will be offered credit and have debts at some point in their lives. At present the UK personal debt totals are close to £1.5 trillion. Many people's largest debt is their mortgage, which is money they have borrowed to buy a house.

If you manage your debt well by paying back the money at the agreed times, you keep reducing your debt until it is paid off and there are no problems. However, if payments are not kept up then serious consequences can arise such as that in Source 1.

Source 1
If you are unable to keep up mortgage payments on your home you would either have to sell your home to pay back the debt and move into a cheaper property or rent; or face having your house taken by your mortgage provider and sold to recover the cost.

ACTIVITY

Why we need credit

2. Make a list of all the different things for which people might be given credit; for example, a mortgage.
3. What problems could arise that would affect people's ability to pay back their debts?

In recent years more and more individuals and businesses have been given credit that they have struggled to pay back. This results in further debt, as additional interest or fines are charged for late repayment. If the debt builds up to a point that the individual or organisation is unable to pay it back they can be declared bankrupt or insolvent. This is likely to have a negative impact on any future credit requests they make.

Source 2

Number of bankruptcies on the rise

More and more individuals and businesses are going bankrupt every day, new figures show.

The number of bankruptcies, both personal and business-related, are increasing at their fastest rate for more than 20 years. Up to 45 companies are being declared bankrupt every day as the credit crunch approaches its third year.

During the period of May–August 2010 more than 4000 firms went into liquidation, which is an increase of 0.5 per cent since the last quarter.

On a personal level, nearly 35,000 people were declared bankrupt during the same period, which is five per cent more than the same period a year ago.

The bankruptcy rate shows that many individuals and businesses are struggling to cope with the effects of the recession and there is a call for banks to lend more to help people through these testing times.

ACTIVITY

The impact of bankruptcy

4. Source 2 shows the problems that thousands of individuals and businesses are facing. One suggestion to help is for banks to lend more.
   a) How would this help?
   b) What potential problems might it result in?
5. Do you know any national or local businesses that have closed down? What is likely to be the impact on:
   a) the owners
   b) the employees and their families?

Source 3 The credit card minimum payment trap

You purchase an item for £1000 using your credit or store card.

Your card has an APR (annual percentage rate – interest) of 18%. This is broken down into 12 monthly periods of 1.5% interest charge per month (18 divided by 12 = 1.5% interest per month).

The minimum payment is 2.5% of the total balance; therefore the minimum payment in the first month would be £25 (£1000 divided by 100 x 2.5 = £25).

This means that only £10 of the £25 actually goes to pay back the £1000 used for the purchase. The other £15 goes to pay back the 1.5% interest (2.5% minimum payment (£25) minus 1.5% interest (£15) = £10).

The next month's statement will show the remaining balance as £990 and the next minimum payment will be calculated at £24.75. The payment will cover the £14.85 interest charge and £9.90 of the actual £1000 purchase cost.

The cycle continues until the debt is paid. In this case assuming that interest rates and other factors stay the same, it would take nearly 13 years (153 months) to pay off the original £1000 debt. £1115.14 would have been paid in interest alone.

Credit cards

Millions of people in the UK have at least one, if not more, credit or store cards. One of the benefits is that they allow you to purchase something that you can't afford to buy outright at the time you want it. If you pay back the balance on your credit card in full each month you are not charged interest – so, in effect, you have been given interest-free credit to buy the item until the credit card bill is due.

However, if you pay back a small minimum amount of the credit each month, you are charged interest on the outstanding balance. This means that you actually end up paying a lot more for the item than what it would have cost if you bought it outright. This can result in being trapped in a cycle of debt that can be very difficult to get out of.

Many competing credit card companies have seen an opportunity to take advantage of people in the debt trap by offering incentives for them to change company, such as:

0% on balance transfers for first 6 months

•••••

6% on balance transfers for 12 months

•••••

10% on balance transfers for the life of the balance

•••••

0% interest on new purchases for 3 months

•••••

0% interest on new purchases for 6 months

These types of offers give people an opportunity to pay back more of the amount they owe. However, it can mean that people have (an) additional credit card(s) and therefore may build up debts again.

The government is keen for people to pay back their borrowing more quickly and cheaply and have suggested introducing new rules, including raising the minimum amount that has to be paid each month from around 2–3% to 5%.

Source 4

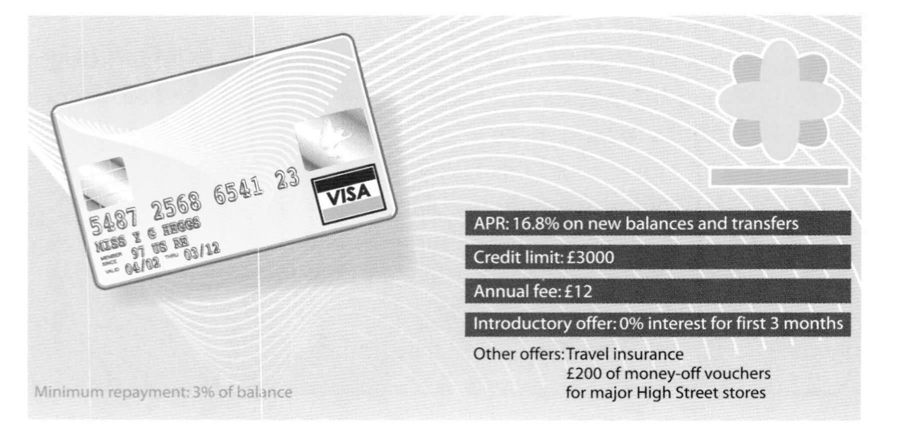

ACTIVITY

Which deal is the best?

6. a) Using the internet or newspapers, search for different offers that are currently available from credit card companies. Look for details such as those in Source 4 and select one credit card that you think offers the best value. Alternatively, you could use the details in Source 4 for this activity.

b) Imagine you are going on a shopping spree. Make a list of all the different things you would buy and their cost, up to the limit of your chosen card.

c) Now, using the APR and minimum payments rates from the card you have chosen, follow the first four steps in the flow chart in Source 3 to find out:

- how much the minimum payment would be in the first month
- how much of that minimum payment is interest, and how much is paying off the original loan.

d) Now work out or estimate the answers to the following questions (use Source 3 to help you). If you only paid the minimum each month:

- how much would you still owe after twelve months
- how much would you end up paying to clear your debt, and how much of this is interest
- how long would it take you to clear the debt
- how long would it take you to clear the debt if you didn't have to make any interest payments?

e) As a class discuss your findings:

- Who had the best credit card deal?
- What problems could people face if they only pay the minimum amount?

ACTIVITY

Pros and cons of credit card use

7. Sort the statements in Source 5 into advantages and disadvantages of using credit or store cards. Add any others you can think of.

8. Make a poster or leaflet informing people about the do's and don'ts of credit card use and strategies for avoiding debt. Research and include information about where people can seek information should they need advice – The Citizens Advice Bureau is a good starting point.

ACTIVITY

Temptation

9. Do you think credit cards provide too much 'temptation' for people?

Source 5 Advantages and disadvantages of credit and store cards

Ease of purchase

Encourage people to spend money they haven't got

High interest rates – minimum payment debt trap

Useful in emergencies

Incentive offers; e.g. air miles or insurance offers

Credit card fraud

Protect your purchases

Help build a good credit history

9 The Future

At what age can I ...?

In this topic you will learn about:

- the multiple roles and responsibilities that people have in society
- the need to manage risk to yourself and others in a range of personal and social situations
- managing money and personal finances.

You will explore:

- a way of recognising your rights and responsibilities
- managing change and transition.

You might not be seen as an adult in the eyes of the law until the age of 18, but as you get older you are legally allowed to do certain things. This can also mean you are legally responsible for your actions. Remember, you have a responsibility to know what you can legally do at your age so it's important to know what's what.

What you can do

This topic tells you at what age you can do things like get a job, buy and drink alcohol, legally have sex, get married or drive different types of vehicles.

Up to this point in your life ...

- At **7** years of age: open a bank account in your own name.
- At **10** years of age: be held criminally responsible (this is age 8 in Scotland).
- At **13** years of age: get a part-time job – with some restrictions.
- At **14** years of age: enter a pub without an adult, but you can't buy or drink alcohol there.

Coming soon ...

At **16** years of age you may:

- buy a lottery ticket
- consent to having sex
- have an abortion without your parents' consent
- consent to or refuse dental or medical treatment
- live independently, subject to certain conditions being met
- get married or have a civil partnership with parental consent
- get a National Insurance number
- ride a moped of up to 50cc
- pilot a glider
- apply for your own passport
- have beer or cider whilst eating a meal in a restaurant or an eating area of a pub as long as you are with someone aged 18 or over, but not in the bar.

In the future...

At **17** years of age you may:

- hold a licence to drive most vehicles
- learn to drive
- buy a car or motorcycle
- be sent to prison
- pilot a plane
- emigrate
- no longer have a Care Order made on you
- leave school.

When you're **18** years of age you are:

- legally seen as an adult in the eyes of the law
- allowed to buy cigarettes and tobacco
- allowed to vote in general and local elections
- allowed to leave home without parental consent
- allowed to get married/have a civil partnership without parental consent
- allowed to open a bank account in your name without a parent or carer's signature
- allowed to buy and drink alcohol in a licensed premises
- allowed to ask to see your birth certificate if you are adopted
- allowed to change your name
- able to be called to serve on a jury
- allowed to sue or be sued
- allowed to make a will
- allowed to place a bet
- allowed to have a tattoo.

Too much too soon?

1. What reasons could you suggest for why a 16-year-old is allowed to pilot a glider but not drive a car?
2. The law says at 10 years old a young person can be held responsible for criminal activity and stand trial for the crime they have committed. Is that too young? Give reasons for your answer.
3. Look at the different ages at which young people are legally allowed to do certain things – is there any specific activity for which you would either raise or lower the age limit? Why?
4. Look at Source 1. What are the arguments for and against raising the age at which people can marry/have a civil partnership?

Source 1

'Til death do us part'?

In 2008 there were just under 122,000 divorces in England and Wales. This number fell for its sixth consecutive year and was the lowest rate for 26 years. One theory for this fall is that people are waiting until they are older to get married in the first place.

The highest percentage of divorces took place for people aged 20–34 and the rate dropped significantly for the over 45s. The average length of marriage for those who got divorced was 11 and a half years.

Money matters ACTIVITY

5. You may open a bank account when you're 7 – but is a 7-year-old really capable of managing their own money? Discuss your answer.
6. Starting with age 7, draw a timeline of when a person, in law, gets other rights associated with financial independence. Use the information on these two pages to help you.
7. With financial independence comes the responsibility to manage money wisely. List two responsibilities you think are needed for this. Share these with a partner and then with a group.

Your opinion ACTIVITY

8. How do you think that the lawmakers who decide these ages should be taking account of young people's opinions? What one piece of advice would you give them?

Moving on

In this topic you will learn about:

- auditing your personal development.

You will explore:

- progress in personal skills and qualities
- hopes and aspirations for the next five years.

ACTIVITY

Looking back

1. The last time you faced a change as big as the one you're facing now (taking public exams and deciding what comes next) you were in primary school. Read Source 1. Think of something that was said about you in primary school that has turned out to be completely right or completely wrong.

Source 1 Looking back on school days

'Ashley is too concerned with maintaining his 'street cred' with others in the class and this has gravely affected his performance in many lessons.'

Footballer Ashley Cole's school report

Sir Isaac Newton's early school reports described him as 'idle' and 'inattentive'.

'Very talkative. Unfortunately what he has to say is not always relevant.'

Comedian Harry Enfield's primary school report

'Is a constant trouble to everybody and is always in some scrape or other.'

Former Prime Minister Sir Winston Churchill's primary school report

'His stubbornness is in his nature, and could be an asset when directed to sound ends. He must learn tact while not losing his outspokenness.'

BBC Newsnight presenter Jeremy Paxman's house master's report

'I was always getting in trouble. Nothing really bad. I didn't like school but I loved drama. I learned about the work ethic, and that applies to my life now more than ever.'

Actor Ashton Kutcher

'We're absolutely delighted with Ellie. She's 100% dedicated and is a great example to pupils.'

Head of Year 9 on Paralympian swimmer Ellie Saunders, BBC Young Sports Personality of the Year and MBE

In preparing for the future you will find it helpful to undertake an audit of what you've achieved so far. Think of how you are developing in personal skills and qualities. Source 2 gives examples of these. Skills and qualities can be equally valuable as qualifications when you're taking part in interviews. Being able to talk about them will help demonstrate that you've thought about your progress and are able to recognise and explain your personal worth.

Source 2

PERSONAL DEVELOPMENT – YOUR SKILLS AND QUALITIES

Your active participation in learning and school life

- developing and defending a point of view
- researching information from a variety of sources
- working positively with others.

Your ability to make informed and responsible choices

- accessing and using formal and informal sources of help
- lifestyle choices; for example, health and well-being
- negotiation and assertiveness skills.

Your self-awareness and self-management

- positive values and attitudes
- qualities and skills you are developing towards your working life
- ability to self-manage.

Your contribution to community life

- member and/or leader of groups
- projects and initiatives that benefit the school and/or wider community
- combating prejudice and discrimination.

ACTIVITY

Taking stock

2. Provide examples to evidence your progress in the areas outlined in Source 2. The example below should help.

Your active participation in learning and school life	
	EXAMPLES
Developing and defending a point of view	Participating in a class debate on the causes of global warming

ACTIVITY

Moving on

4. If you could do or be anything you wanted to, where would your ambition lead?

ACTIVITY

Looking forward

3. One way of managing your life as things are changing is to visualise a positive future for yourself. Write a letter to yourself about what you are hoping for and where you want to be in five years' time. Here are some questions to consider:

- Do I have an idea of a career or job I want to do?
- Do I want to continue in full/part-time study?
- How will I finance the things I want; for example, clothes, holidays, entertainment?
- Can I combine both studying and working?
- Your friends or you may be leaving school soon – how will that affect you?
- When will it be the right time to leave home and move out (see Source 3)?

Source 3

Leaving home at 18?

There are no hard and fast rules about leaving home … for some people it's a great idea; for others, it's not so great at all.

It also depends on your individual situation. Some 18-year-olds are at university and still financially dependent on their families. If that's the case, then it can be tough to get a flat of your own …

Some people may have left school at 16 and have been working for a couple of years. Although they may have more financial independence than their uni-bound counterparts, that doesn't mean they are emotionally ready to be living on their own.

It's important to consider if you feel emotionally ready to leave, can afford the extra living expenses and are willing to take on the extra responsibilities of living away from home. At the same time, leaving home doesn't mean your family will want nothing more to do with you. Hopefully they will still be there to lend support and the door will always be open to you.

Life isn't a race, and no one will think less of you if you opt to live at home.

Adapted from www.thesite.org

Study or employment – what's out there?

In this topic you will learn about:

- the different pathways that are available at the end of Year 11
- where you can find information about future pathway options
- risks associated with the different pathways.

You will explore:

- questions you need to consider when thinking about future options
- advantages and disadvantages of different pathways.

As you get towards the end of Year 11, you will have some difficult decisions to make about your future. The decisions you make at this point will start you on your career path so it is important to know what options are available to you.

There are four main pathways you could follow, as shown in the diagram below.

Source 1 Pathways

Finish compulsory education or training

Pathway 1: Full-time education

You can continue in full-time education by continuing in sixth form. As well as A levels you can choose from a range of work-related qualifications or diplomas.

Pathway 2: Work-based training/learning

If you want to start work, many jobs will offer planned training that leads to nationally recognised qualifications, such as, diplomas and BTECs in carpentry and floristry.

Pathway 3: Full-time employment

You could enter full-time employment that has a regular income and training but does not necessarily lead to nationally recognised qualifications.

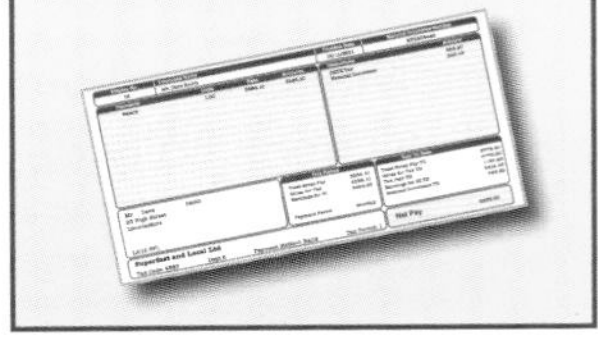

Pathway 4: Time out

Some students decide to take time out to gain experience in other areas. This might include travelling, work experience or voluntary work.

University

You may decide to go to university to study; this will give you even more options when you come to seek employment.

Having gained further qualifications you could now follow Pathway 2, 3 or 4. The qualifications you have gained will mean that you have more options when seeking employment and your earnings may be higher.

Having taken 'time out' you will be able to proceed on Pathways 1–3. Your decision may be influenced by what you did during your time out. You may decide to go to university after taking a year out from completing your sixth form or college course.

ACTIVITY

What are my options?

1. a) Using the information in Source 1, draw your own flow diagram that shows the pathway you might follow. Include as much detail as you can; for example, you could include the name of a college, specific subjects you would like to study or types of voluntary work. Your teachers will be able to provide further information, as will careers advisors and school and college websites. An example of a flow diagram is given below.

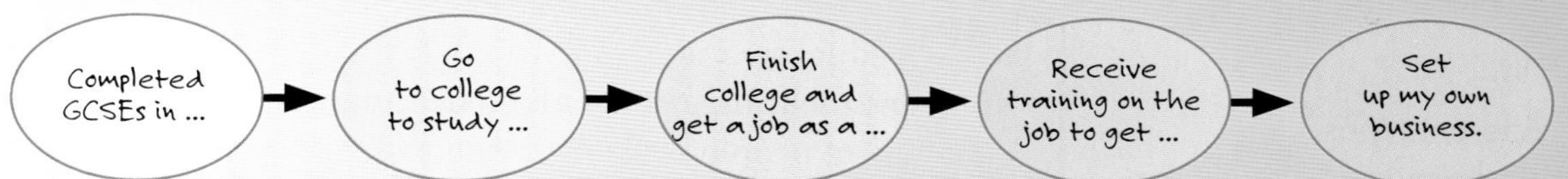

b) You may find that some sections of your flow diagram are more difficult than others to complete as you don't yet have the information you need. Make a list of all the questions you need answers to in order to add further detail to your flow diagram; for example: What courses are available at my local college? How would I be expected to travel there? If I went into an apprenticeship, how much would learn?

c) In groups, discuss your questions with each other to see if anyone has similar questions, or if anyone is able to help you answer the questions you have.

d) As a class, make a list of the questions that still remain unanswered. Discuss who or which organisations would be able to provide the information needed.

e) From your list of questions, select three that are of interest to you. Make a note of these and over the next week see if you can find the answers to them. Feed back in your next lesson what you have found.

Risks

Any pathway you choose comes with risks, both financially and in terms of your overall career progression. The trick is to weigh up the advantages and disadvantages of each pathway whilst considering the type of person you are; for example, if you are someone who enjoys school, a sixth-form course may be more suitable; if you haven't really enjoyed your school life but do want to have additional training, you may choose work-related training. Remember it is what best suits you!

ACTIVITY

What are the risks?

2. Make a copy of the table below. Using the information in Source 2, fill in the table to show the advantages and disadvantages of each pathway option (some of the advantages and disadvantages could relate to more than one option). Add any others you can think of.

	Full-time education	Work-related training	Full-time employment	Time out
Advantages				
Disadvantages				

Source 2 Pros and cons

- **a.** Could lead to a large debt
- **b.** Earn straight away
- **c.** Higher qualifications to put on CV
- **d.** Increased competition as more students apply
- **e.** Keep options open
- **f.** Leads to a skilled trade/ profession
- **g.** Less chance for promotion
- **h.** Likely to lead to a higher paid job
- **i.** LOW/NO INCOME
- **j.** Lower earnings
- **k.** lower pay until qualified
- **l.** More employment options open to you
- **m.** Most friends follow a different pathway
- **n.** Nationally recognised qualifications
- **o.** VALUABLE EXPERIENCES; FOR EXAMPLE, TRAVELLING

10 Employability

Types of employment and employment trends

In this topic you will learn about:

- different types of employment opportunities that are available
- how financial issues will influence your choice of future employment
- how employment patterns and trends are changing.

You will explore:

- the advantages and disadvantages of different types of employment
- how external factors could affect your employment decisions.

Job, occupation, career, vocation, employment and work are all terms commonly used to describe what is expected of us when our formal education is over. Although these terms do have slightly different meanings, they all basically refer to the fact that the majority of people will enter 'the world of work' when their formal education is at its end.

'The world of work' will be different for everyone and, to begin with, this is dependent largely on what has been achieved during formal education.

The types of work people do can be split into three main categories:

Employed

A person who is employed is known as an 'employee'. They will work for an individual or company and receive a wage or salary. The majority of people in work are employees.

Self-employed

A person who is self-employed will work for themselves and keep track of their own earnings. It is likely that they will be highly skilled, perhaps in a trade such as plumbing, or they will have a niche product to offer.

Voluntary work

A voluntary worker is a person who doesn't get paid for the services they offer. They are often associated with charity and support work, but could actually be involved in a wide range of work.

Each type of employment has advantages and disadvantages that need to be considered before entering into the 'world of work'. Some of these are shown in Source 2.

Types of employment

1. a) Under the headings 'Employed', 'Self-employed' and 'Voluntary', put the jobs shown in Source 1 into the correct category (some could fall in more than one – explain why, when this is the case). Add to your lists so that for each category you have eight different jobs.
   b) Look through your lists and highlight the jobs in each list that you would most like to do if you had to choose.
   c) Now work with a partner and explain to them the reasons why you highlighted your particular jobs. Were you partner's reasons for choosing their jobs the same as yours?

Source 1 Different jobs

a) Solicitor

b) Accountant

c) Lifeguard

d) Farmer

e) Firefighter

f) Television producer

g) Working in a soup kitchen

h) Dressmaker

i) Removal person

j) Software engineer

k) Plumber

l) Environmental worker

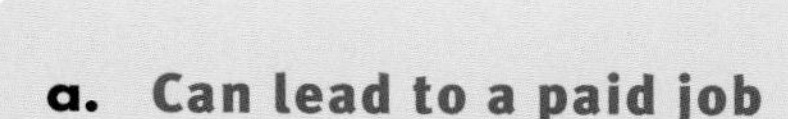

Source 2 Advantages and disadvantages

a. **Can lead to a paid job**

b. **Childcare costs**

c. Decide own pay

d. *Flexible working hours*

e. **Guaranteed income**

f. Hours to suit

g. Job satisfaction

h. **Lack of appreciation**

i. *Monitored performance*

j. No income

k. *No sick pay*

l. Own boss

m. Paid holiday

n. **Pension paid**

o. *Set-up costs*

p. Time-consuming

q. UNPAID HOLIDAY

r. **Workers' rights**

Pros and cons

2. Make a copy of the table below. Look at the advantages and disadvantages in Source 2 and put them where you think they should go in your table. Some could be used more than once.

	Employed	Self-employed	Voluntary
Advantages			
Disadvantages			

Career paths

There are many factors that influence someone's work or career choice. These include interests and resulting job satisfaction; whether you have the appropriate skills and qualities to match the job (see pages 103–105); and the amount of money you can earn and potential future earnings.

For most people entering the 'world of work' for the first time, there is a long and hard pathway in front of them before they can earn the amount of money they would like. You have to 'work your way up' in terms of your training, experience, references and eventually earnings. This is known as the 'career path'; and it begins in school. The better the results you achieve in school and the longer you stay in education, including sixth form and university, the more opportunities you are likely to have to follow a 'career path' that leads to a higher paid job (see page 105).

In addition to your success in education, economic issues will also impact on your opportunities to achieve your aspirations.

Credit crunch

The 'credit crunch' that started in 2007 has seen small businesses collapse, larger businesses make employees redundant and society as a whole 'tighten its belt'. As a result, the career opportunities available to students when they finished school dried up and unemployment levels rose. Higher unemployment means that people have less money to spend, demand for goods and services drops and the government receives less money through taxes, but still has to spend money on services such as health and education. This can result in large spending cuts, which can affect everyone.

As a result of limited employment opportunities during the 'credit crunch' the number of students applying for university places increased. In August 2010 record numbers of students applied for university despite the fact that they have to pay tuition fees and are likely to leave university with an average debt of £18,000–£25,000. It was reported that 150,000 students didn't get a university place.

Source 3 shows unemployment rates from 1992 to 2010. As you can see the number of people unemployed has generally gone down, until 2008 when the 'credit crunch' had begun. Using graphs such as this we are able to work out **employment trends**. If we looked at statistics dating back even further we would notice that unemployment rates rise and fall many times.

Source 3 Unemployment in the UK 1992–2010

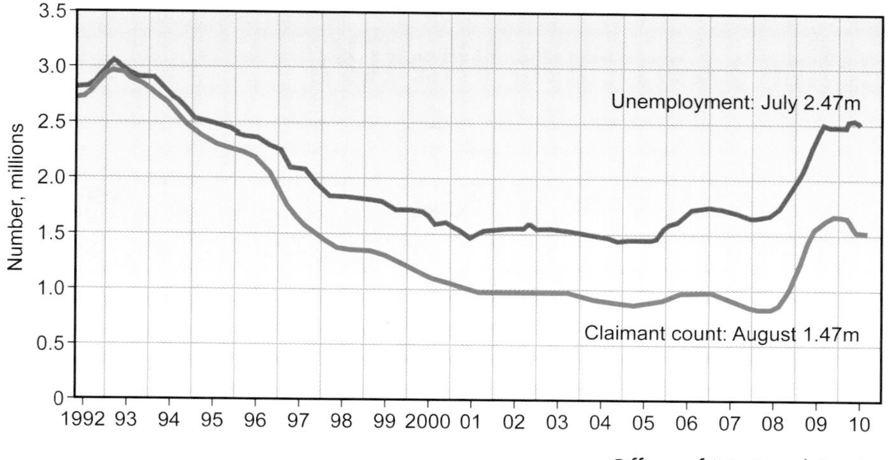

Office of National Statistics

So what is likely to happen? We know that as the economy recovers more jobs will be created and unemployment rates will come down, but what are the key trends in employment at the moment and how might they change in the future?

Source 4 Employment trends

a) In the next ten years (from 2010) the government predicts that employee jobs will grow steadily and that self-employment will increase rapidly.

b) It is estimated that around two-thirds of the new jobs will go to women and that around two-thirds of all the new jobs will be part-time.

c) It is estimated that nearly three million new jobs will be created in the services sector (both private and public), some in well-paid professional jobs but also a great many in lower-paid service-sector jobs.

d) Most workers will have between 20 and 25 jobs in their working lives.

e) One in four employees will stay with their employer for less than a year, whilst one in two will stay for less than five years.

f) The top ten jobs in 2015 don't yet exist, as new industries and problems will see the creation of new jobs.

a)–c) from www.tuc.org.uk/changingtimes/worktrends.htm

Employment trends ACTIVITY

3. Select four of the boxes about employment trends in Source 4 and for each one think of a reason/reasons why this trend is likely to happen.

Funding for the future ACTIVITY

4. The government has recently announced in their spending cuts that Year 12 and 13 students will no longer be able to apply for the Educational Maintenance Allowance (EMA). This funding was initially set up to encourage students from lower income families to stay in school and complete A levels or equivalent. As a result of these cuts, thousands of students up and down the country have protested through marches, petitions and other protest methods.
Do you think the government was right to cut EMA funding? Consider the present financial situation the country is in, and also your own future.

Your future ACTIVITY

5. Using the information you have learned in this topic, write a paragraph explaining how your own future could be affected. You need to consider the following factors:
- the type of employment you may enter into
- how your education could influence this
- the cost of your education and who pays
- unemployment rates
- future employment trends.

Creating a Curriculum Vitæ (CV)

In this topic you will learn about:

- effective ways to present personal information
- the essentials for creating your own Curriculum Vitæ (CV).

You will explore:

- how to compile your own CV
- how to compare your CV with those of other people.

When applying for a job (even a part-time one) your prospective employer will probably want to get a sense of what kind of person you are. You are often asked to send in your **Curriculum Vitæ (CV)** or complete an application form, which as well as including contact details, qualifications and work experience should also include some of the personal hobbies and interests you have. This is important as it gives the employer some indication of what you are like.

Source 1 Good … better … best!

Jane is preparing a list of her personal hobbies and interests for a job application. Here are three ways she could describe her interests. They are all true – but the third one is the best.

- Reading, cinema, keeping a scrapbook, crafting.

These interests could imply she is a solitary individual who doesn't get on with other people. This may not be true, but an employer will draw their first conclusions from what they read in an application.

- Reading, cinema, keeping in touch with my 'exchange' friend, socialising.

This sounds a little better – Jane is beginning to look like somebody who can get on with other people.

- Cinema: member of the school film club.
  Travel: had a summer on 'exchange' – visited historic sites and practised my French and Spanish with the family and friendship group there.
  Reading: helped younger pupils with reading difficulties at school.

Jane is still the same individual as in the first example, but here the impression is completely the opposite – her interests show she is an outgoing, proactive individual who helps others.

ACTIVITY

The best of me

1. a) Look at Source 1. Why do you think an employer might be more favourable to the third example?
   b) What's the best way to describe your interests? First brainstorm a list of words to identify your interests, then work in pairs to write a bullet list that outlines your hobbies and activities in an interesting and useful way – remember you want to make a prospective employer interview you.

What is a CV?

A **Curriculum Vitæ (CV)** is an outline of a person's education and work experience. (It means, literally, 'the course of one's life'.) It is usually prepared for job applications. Another name for a CV is a résumé.

A CV is the most flexible and convenient way to make applications. It should convey your personal details in a way that presents you in the best possible light. It is useful to leave a copy with the people you're hoping to get a job with; for example, when you're asking around for a weekend/holiday job.

Sometimes employers ask for an application form instead. This is designed to bring out the essential information and personal qualities that the employer requires. Having prepared a CV (even though you can't submit it) can save you time when filling out these forms as all the information about you is already set out in one place.

There is no 'one best way' to construct a CV; it is your document and can be structured as you wish within a basic framework. You could send it in on paper or complete it online if that is what the employer asks for. If you're applying for something particularly creative you may find another way to present your CV; for example, a Facebook profile or a blog page!

Source 2 on the following page shows an example of a 16-year-old student's CV with comments that highlight and explain its different aspects.

ACTIVITY

My CV

2. Compile your own CV. Look at Source 2 on the following page and try and follow the good advice for setting out your skills and experience. Use the interests you identified in Activity 1b) in your CV.
3. Work with someone else and look at each other's CV. Identify areas for improvement in light of the advice given in Source 2 on the following page and make suggestions to help the other person.

ACTIVITY

Further research

4. Ask family friends and relatives for copies of their CVs so that you can compare and contrast different ways of setting them out. You could use templates from programs such as Word to practise various layouts.

Source 2

Nick Alexander: Curriculum Vitæ

4 Somewhere Close, Weald Gate, HA24 7PE
Phone: 020 0031 7245 (home) 06752 932 100 (mobile)
Email: nick@nicksworld.com
Nationality: British
Age: 16 (on 15 June 2011)

Include your name, address, date of birth (although with age discrimination laws now in force this isn't essential), telephone number and email.

Achievements and interests

- Attended Weald Gate High School for the past five years and have every intention of entering the sixth form in September 2011.
- I currently help younger pupils, in Year 7, with reading support.
- Captain of school tennis team.
- Whilst a student in Year 9 I attended an international camp in Spain where I continued my National Curriculum education alongside pupils from South America, Russia and European countries. The experience was invaluable in terms of gaining responsibility, independence and the confidence to communicate and interact even when there was a language barrier.
- My hobbies include skiing, tennis, working out at the gym, cinema and theatre.

Keep this section short and to the point. Bullets can be used to separate the text.

Anything showing evidence of employability skills. Here Nick has shown he can work with others.

Any evidence of leadership is important to mention, e.g. captain or coach of a sports team.

Include extra curricular activities and life experiences that are relevant for future work.

Don't include many passive, solitary hobbies – show a range of interests to avoid coming across as narrow. If everything centres around only one type of activity they may wonder if your focus is too narrow or you need more life experiences.

Work experience/Employment

2010 – Kutz Hair and Beauty Salon, High Road, Weald Gate, Hampdenshire
As a 'junior' I undertook duties that ranged from cleaning the salon, making coffee for staff and clients, washing hair and working on reception to cover absences and breaks.

2011 – The Elms Tennis and Football Club, Weald Close, Weald Gate, Hampdenshire
I helped organise and lead a team who supported children aged 5–13 years in playing games, and learning to play tennis. My responsibilities also included pastoral welfare at break and lunchtimes.

Work in a shop, bar or restaurant will involve working in a team, providing a quality service to customers and dealing tactfully with complaints.

Try to relate the skills to the job. Nick has prepared this CV for a position working with young people.

Nick uses action words such as 'organise' and 'lead'.

Education and qualifications

2006–2011 Weald Gate High School

GCSE subjects:
Art; English; ICT; French; Maths;
Physical Education; Religious Studies; Science

Your subjects can also highlight your skills, such as languages and computing.

By the time Nick is 21 this will include his degree subject and university, plus A levels and GCSEs or equivalents. Mention grades unless poor!

References

Frank Byers	Virginia Lawn
Owner/MD	Managing Director
Kutz Hair and Beauty Salon	The Elms Tennis and Football Club
High Road	Weald Close
Weald Gate	Weald Gate
Hampdenshire	Hampdenshire
Tel: 020 0031 7322	Tel: 020 0031 8787

Usually two references are sufficient. These could be from school and from an employer (perhaps your last part-time or summer job).

Skills and qualities needed for employment

In this topic you will learn about:

- the importance of qualifications and qualities
- the personal qualities that contribute to employability.

You will explore:

- your own qualities, and receive feedback from others
- the skills and qualifications needed for future employment.

ACTIVITY

The world is your oyster

1. What do you think the saying 'the world is your oyster' means?

For someone to make the world their oyster they need to be able to develop their skills and qualities in order to achieve as much as they possibly can. Read Source 1 – Junior Apprentice. Some of you may have followed Arjun's progress on *Junior Apprentice*.

Source 1 Junior Apprentice

- In 2010 became the first winner of Junior Apprentice, aged 17
- Prize was £25,000 fund to go towards his business career
- In 2010 was studying A-Levels in Physics, Maths, Systems and Control and an AS in Further Maths, and running a computer repair business from home
- Arjun says 'Always look at the end goal and find a way to get there.'
- 'A worthy winner. Level-headed well beyond his 17 years, likeable, diplomatic and king of the surprised facial expression. For once the right person won.' Julia Raeside, *The Guardian*

Arjun Rajyagor, winner of *Junior Apprentice*, 2010.

ACTIVITY

Striking a balance

2. Arjun's outline shows a balance between qualifications, skills and qualities. Can you identify one of these for Arjun in each case?

Qualifications and qualities

What's the difference?

3. a) What's the difference between a qualification, a skill and a quality?

b) A vet will have to have particular qualifications (see below). But what qualities would it be good for a vet to have?

In order to practise veterinary medicine in the UK most vets will be members of the Royal College of Veterinary Surgeons (RCVS). They will need a degree from a university recognised by the RCVS or to have passed the MRCVS examination.

We can see that everyone needs more than just qualifications and skills to make the most of their lives. Each of us has qualities that we use socially and in the world of work. In addition to assessing your skills and abilities you also need to be able to recognise and reflect on your personal qualities. This will help you when thinking about your future career plans.

Source 2 Personal qualities – an alphabetical list

a) Careful – you take care of your own and others' feelings
b) Courageous – you stand up for what you believe in and don't shrink away from challenges
c) Creative and original – you are an innovative thinker and full of new ideas
d) Critical thinker – you think things through before taking action
e) Curious and interested – you like exploration and discovering new things
f) Enthusiastic and energetic – you approach projects with excitement and energy
g) Fair and principled – you do not let your personal feelings bias your decisions
h) Good team player – you always do your share and work hard for the group
i) Hard worker – you don't get distracted and you meet your deadlines
j) Honest and genuine – you are down-to-earth and try to be yourself
k) Kind and generous – you enjoy doing things for other people and are willing to offer time and help
l) Leader – you are a good organiser and will encourage everyone in the group to get things done

ACTIVITY

Personal qualities

4. Look at Source 2 and score yourself against the list: A score of 5 means that you are strong in the quality. A score of 1 means you do not have much of this quality in you.

Source 3 Websites for self-assessment

www.direct.gov.uk

www.connexions-direct.com/jobs4u

Further ways to self-assess

5. The websites featured in Source 3 are a starting point when thinking about future careers. Explore these to help you identify the types of skills and qualifications you will need to develop for the career path you would like to follow.
6. What are the qualities you need to develop in order to help you achieve what you want to in the future?

ACTIVITY

Self-reflection

7. Complete this sentence: One new thing I've learned about myself today is...

Rights and responsibilities at work

In this topic you will learn about:

- relationships between employers and employees
- what trade unions are and how they protect their members.

You will explore:

- the rights that all employees have at work
- the expectation employers have of their employees
- methods used by trade unions to support their members.

Regardless of the work you do there are certain rights and responsibilities that all employers and employees have.

Within the UK, clear employment laws are in place that set out specific rights that have associated responsibilities for both employers and employees (see Source 1).

Source 1 The responsible employer

An employer must:

- give their employees a contract of employment that sets out terms and conditions such as pay, hours, holidays, the type of job you will do and the leave period you need to give or can expect to receive when your employment ends
- provide employees with an itemised pay slip (see page 82)
- pay employees at least the national minimum wage
- give men and women the same pay for doing the same job
- give part-time and full-time workers the same rights
- give employees reasonable time off for specific events such as family emergencies
- give employees paid holiday
- give women time off during pregnancy for antenatal care and up to 52 weeks' maternity leave
- give parents unpaid time off as appropriate to be with their young children, particularly if the children are under 5 or have disabilities
- follow health and safety guidelines as laid out by government law and EU directives
- give statutory sick pay to those who are entitled
- give redundancy pay to workers who have been at a company for at least two years and are laid off
- treat all workers the same regardless of gender, race or disabilities.

The employer has a great deal of responsibility to ensure that all the rights of the employee are met. However, employment is a 'two-way' thing and the employee also has responsibilities.

ACTIVITY

Responsibilities

1. **a)** Make a list of all the different responsibilities you think an employee should have; for example, being punctual and starting work on time.
   b) Go through your list. Highlight which are also appropriate to you at school.
2. Discuss the following questions:
   a) Are you always as responsible as you should be in school? If not, why not? If yes, why do you think it is important to be responsible?
   b) What happens when someone behaves irresponsibly at school? What is likely to happen if someone behaves irresponsibly at work? Are there any differences?

Although employees are protected by employment laws, many employees also choose to join a **trade union**, which offers them further 'protection' at work.

The main aims of trade unions are to:

- **negotiate agreements with employers on pay and conditions**
- **discuss major changes to the workplace, such as large-scale redundancy**
- **discuss their members' concerns with employers**
- **accompany their members in disciplinary and grievance meetings**
- **provide their members with legal and financial advice**
- **provide education facilities and certain consumer benefits, such as discounted insurance.**

www.direct.gov.uk

There are occasions when union members may vote to strike if they feel that compromises with their employer aren't being reached. Source 2 shows some details of a strike that took place in 2010.

Unions and strike action

3. Why are trade unions important for employees when we already have employment laws that are in place to protect workers?
4. Read Source 2. What would be the impact of strike action by British Airways cabin crew?
5. Most of the teachers in your school will be part of a union. What would be the impact (both short and long-term) if they voted to strike over pay and conditions?
6. Can you think of any jobs in which workers might not be allowed to strike? Why would they not be allowed?
7. The organisation the National Union of Students (NUS) is a union set up for students. Imagine that you are setting up a student union in your school. Produce a leaflet/poster/manifesto outlining what you stand for, what services you would provide, and the rights and responsibilities students, staff and the school have. The NUS website may help you with some ideas – www.nus.org.uk.

Source 2

British Airways Cabin Crew Strike 2010

British Airways cabin crew voted by an overwhelming majority (80% of votes) to take strike action following a failure in negotiations between British Airways management and Unite, the trade union representing them. The strike is over changes to pay, conditions and staffing levels. BA has threatened to take away travel perks from its employees if the strikes go ahead.

The strike action will cause major disruption as hundreds of flights are cancelled leaving thousands of passengers delayed or needing to find alternative travel arrangements.

ACTIVITY

Just a minute

8. In pairs play a game of 'just a minute'. You must talk for one minute about rights and responsibilities at work without pausing or hesitating. Your partner needs to listen carefully to see if you repeat yourself. Once you have had a go swap with your partner.

Employment opportunities

In this topic you will learn about:

- local, national, European and global employment opportunities
- different ways you can search for work
- the different factors to consider when seeking work abroad.

You will explore:

- types of jobs that are available in different locations
- useful places to search when looking for employment
- the pros and cons of working abroad.

The 'world of work' has changed rapidly over the last 15 years and is continuing to do so. One of the main reasons for this is the development of high-speed internet and mobile communications, which means that ideas and information can be shared instantly at the touch of a button.

Another way in which things have changed is where people choose to work. As a result of improvements in communication, transport and trade relations, businesses have been able to set up all over the world and employees have been given the same opportunities.

When looking for work it is important not only to know what is available, but also where. To fulfil your career aspirations you may find that you need to move in order to get the job you desire.

ACTIVITY

Categories of work

1. a) Using a selection of local newspapers, look through the jobs sections and make a note of how many jobs you find in each of the categories in Source 1.

b) Discuss the following questions.

- Which category of job was the most and which was the least common?
- What does this activity tell you about the local labour market?
- Which jobs are most likely to be there in the future? Why?
- Which jobs are most likely to disappear in the future? Why?
- Are there any jobs that you have found that are of interest to you? If yes, explain why you are interested in them; if no, explain what type of job you are interested in and why.
- Where else could you get information about local jobs?

Source 1 CRCI (Connexions Resource Centre Index) occupational families

- Administration, business and office work
- Building and construction
- Catering and hospitality
- Computers and IT
- Design, art and crafts
- Healthcare
- Education and training
- Engineering
- Environment, animals and plants
- Financial services
- Personal and other services including hair and beauty
- Languages, information and culture
- Legal and political services
- Leisure and sport
- Manufacturing
- Retail, sales and customer services
- Marketing and advertising
- Media, print and publishing
- Performing arts
- Science, mathematics and statistics
- Security and armed forces
- Social work and counselling services
- Transport and logistics

If you are unable to find a job that interests you locally, you may need to consider looking further afield.

Looking for work

2. a) Go to www.direct.gov.uk/en/Employment/Jobseekers/LookingForWork/index.htm. Click on 'Find a job now' and then 'Search for a job'. Simply type in a job that is of interest to you and click 'Search'. You will be presented with a list of jobs from all over the country. Glance through the list and click on any that take your interest.

b) Choose ten different jobs, and for each one mark their location on a map of the UK. You may need to use an atlas to help you find the different locations. Next to each location write down what the job is, wages and any other key information.

c) In small groups discuss the locations you have found for your particular job. Would you be prepared to move? Are you likely to find the same job locally? How would you feel if you had to move away from family and friends?

Working in Europe

Being British automatically makes you a European citizen, which means that you are entitled to travel, work and live anywhere within the European Union. This gives you more opportunity to seek out the jobs you are looking for or relocate if you want a change of lifestyle or surroundings.

The map in Source 2 shows the number of UK nationals who worked in other EU countries in September 2008.

Source 2 Number of UK nationals working in EU countries, September 2008

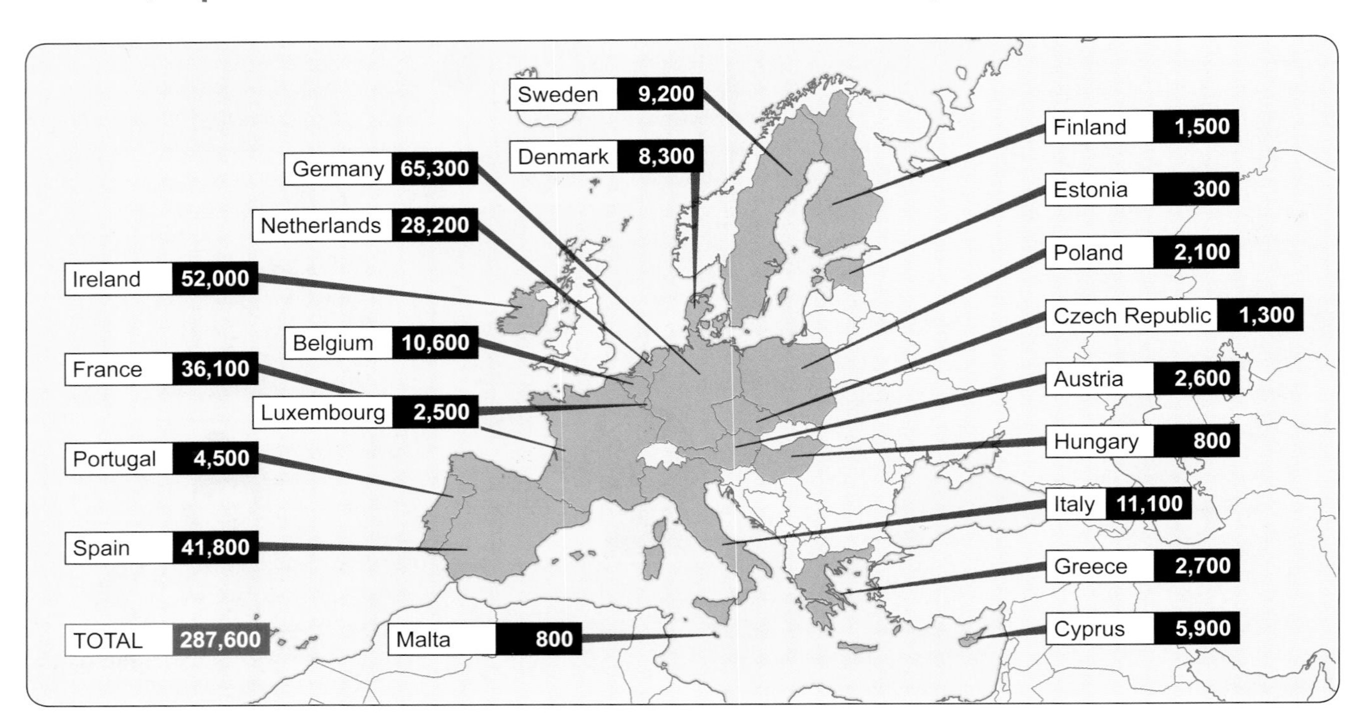

Working in Europe

3. Source 2 shows that the number of British people working in Europe is not evenly distributed. Give reasons why more British people choose to work in Germany, Ireland, Spain, France and the Netherlands than any other European countries.

4. Using the internet, go to www.eurojobs.com. Think back to the jobs you looked at in Activity 2 (page 109) and use the website to search for similar jobs. Are the details similar?

5. What incentives would you need to pack up, leave Britain and work in a European country? Discuss you reasons in pairs.

Migration

Being a member of the European Union also means that people from other member countries can seek employment in the UK. You may have read or heard headlines such as those on the following page.

Eastern Europeans taking our jobs

How many more can we take?

Cheap labour costs us jobs

Migrant workers out of control

The fact is that the headlines simply don't give the full story. The truth is that we need workers from other countries to fill the shortage of skills and labour in different areas of the labour market, ranging from doctors and dentists, to farm labourers.

Working beyond Europe

If you are unable to find the job or lifestyle you want within Britain or other European Union countries, you may decide to look further afield. With transport and communication being as good as they are today, people now have the whole world in which to seek employment opportunities.

The process of being able to work in countries outside of the European Union is more complex. You are likely to need documents such as visas and work permits, have a minimum amount of money in your bank account, have medical checks and also be given injections against certain illnesses before you are allowed to move.

Despite the complex processes, the potential rewards for working beyond the EU can be huge, not only financially but also in terms of satisfaction.

It is now estimated that 5.5 million British people live and work permanently throughout the world – almost one in 10 of the UK population. The top five countries can be seen in the table below – what do they all have in common?

Country name	Resident Britons
Australia	1,300,000
United States	678,000
Canada	603,000
New Zealand	215,000
South Africa	212,000

ACTIVITY

Migration, media and prejudice

6. a) Why do you think that newspapers and other media sources write such provocative headlines as those above?

b) What is the likely impact on the individuals and communities being referred to in such headlines?

ACTIVITY

Working across the world

7. Make a list of all the positive and negative factors of moving outside of the EU to work.

ACTIVITY

What about you?

8. a) Can you ever see yourself moving away from your local area to work? If so, how far do you think you are likely to go – national, European or global?

b) Do you think your attitude will change with time? Explain your answer.

11 Business and Enterprise

Business structure and organisation

In this topic you will learn about:

- different types of business structure
- how well-known businesses are structured
- how business structures can be organised.

You will explore:

- the advantages and disadvantages of tall and flat business structures
- how businesses are structured and organised depending on their product/service
- the structure and organisation of your school.

ACTIVITY

What makes a successful product?

1. a) Make a list of the latest gadgets you have bought recently or would like to buy.

b) Choose one from your list and give reasons why you think it has become so successful.

c) Speak to two other people in your class to find out what product they chose and the reasons they think their product became successful. Were their reasons for the product's success the same as yours?

Businesses come in all shapes and sizes and offer a wide range of products and services. The overall aim of a business is to make more money than it spends. This is known as '**profit**'.

Some of the reasons for success you may have come up with in Activity 1 are: the use of new technology; successful marketing; low costs; or solves a significant problem. You may or may not have thought about how the businesses that produce the products are organised. But the organisation and structure of any business is just as essential for success as the idea, product or service offered.

Business structures

Most businesses are structured in one of two main ways, usually depending on their size. Both have their advantages and disadvantages.

1. Tall (hierarchical)

In a tall organisation, employees are ranked at different levels, each one above another. At each level, except the bottom, one person has a team of people reporting to them. Source 1 shows a diagram illustrating this type of structure and Source 2 outlines some advantages and disadvantages of this way of organising a business.

Source 1 The tall structure

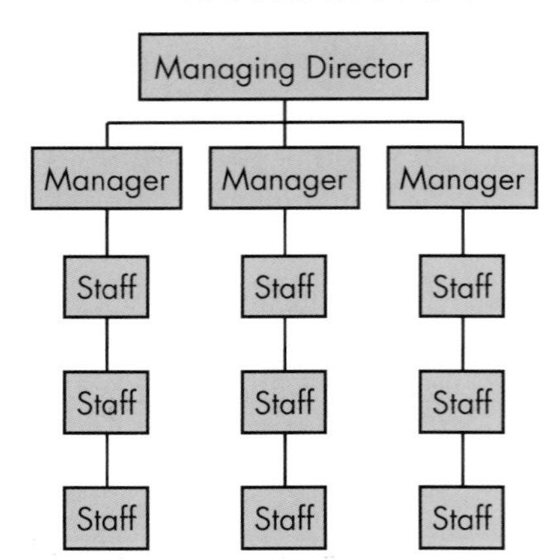

Source 2 Advantages and disadvantages of the tall structure

Advantages	Disadvantages
Each manager has a small number of employees under their control. This means that employees can be closely supervised.	The freedom and responsibility of employees is restricted.
There is a clear management structure.	Decision-making could be slowed down as approval may be needed by each of the layers of authority.
The function of each layer will be clear and distinct. There will be clear lines of responsibility and control.	Communication has to take place through many layers of management.
There is a clear progression and promotion ladder.	There are high management costs because managers are generally paid more than subordinates. Each layer will tend to pay its managers more money than the layer below it.

2. Flat

In a flat hierarchy, the chain of command is much shorter (fewer layers) and the span of control wider. Source 3 shows a diagram illustrating this type of structure and Source 4 outlines some advantages and disadvantages of this way of organising a business.

Source 3 The flat structure

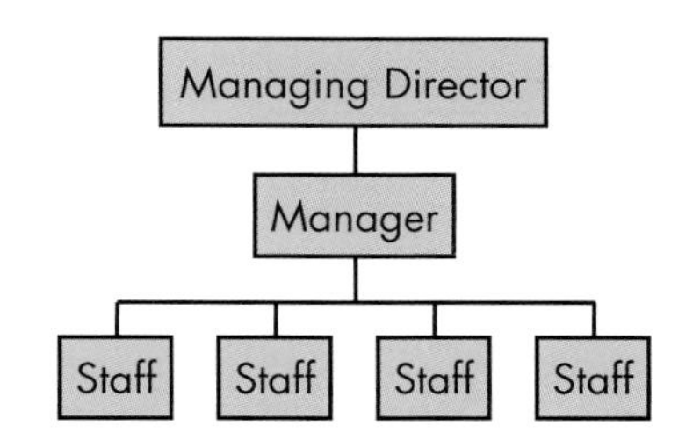

Source 4 Advantages and disadvantages of the flat structure

Advantages	Disadvantages
More/greater communication between management and workers.	Workers may have more than one manager/boss.
Better team spirit.	May limit/hinder the growth of the organisation.
Less bureaucracy and easier decision-making.	Structure usually limited to small organisations.
Fewer levels of management, which includes benefits such as lower costs, as managers are generally paid more.	Function of each department/person could be blurred and merge into the job roles of others.

Other types of business structure include **centralised**, **collaborative** and **matrix**.

ACTIVITY

Which is the right type of business structure?

2. Using the information from sources 1–4 on these two pages, produce two spidergrams showing the advantages and disadvantages of the two main types of business structure.

3. a) Choose one of the well-known companies on the right. Use the internet to research the type of business structure it uses. Before you carry out your research, try and predict the type of business structure you would expect the company to use based on what you know about the company already. Were you right?

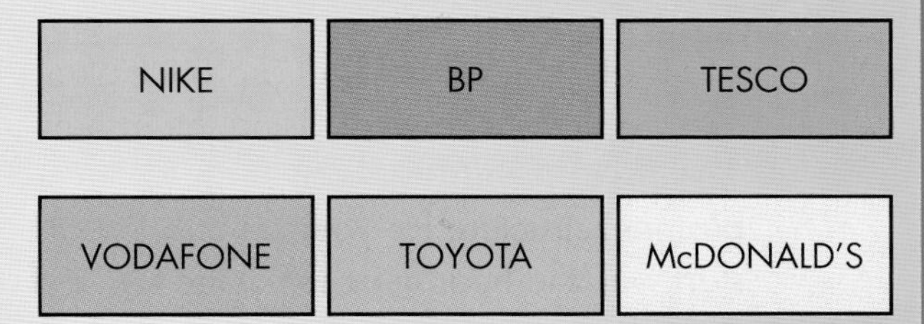

b) Discuss your findings as a class:
- Is there one business structure that is more common than the others?
- If so, why do you think this is?
- Why do you think an appropriate business structure is so important?

4. What type of business structure does your school use and why?

Business organisations

Each business will organise its structure to increase its efficiency and productivity. Different types of organisation can be seen in Sources 5–8.

Source 5 Organisation by function

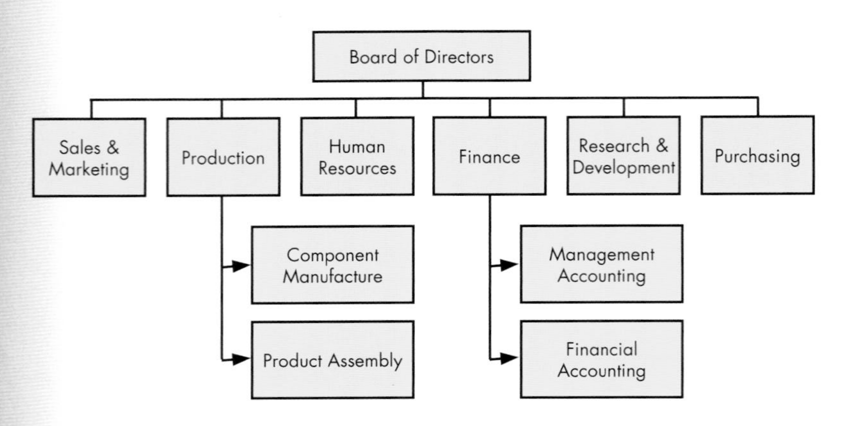

Source 6 Organisation by product

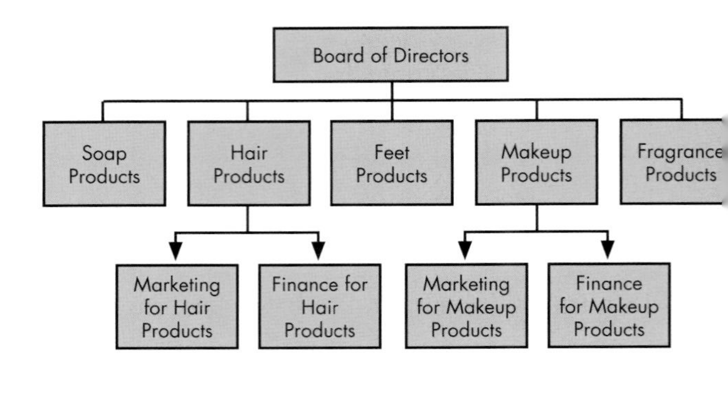

Source 7 Organisation by area/region

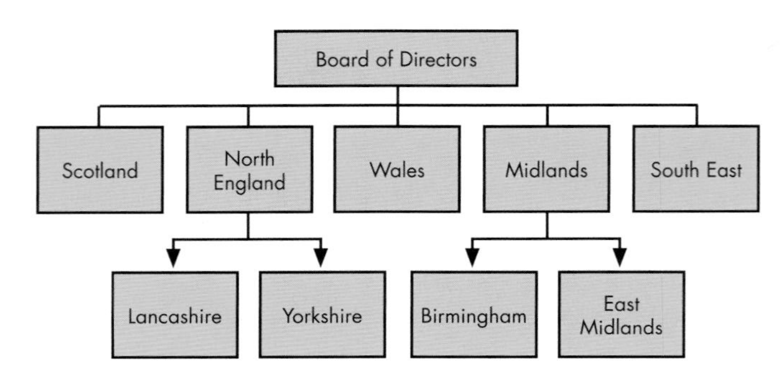

Source 8 Organisation by process

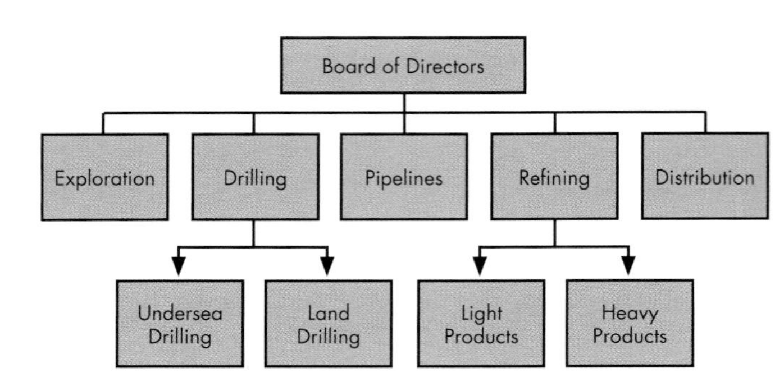

ACTIVITY

Organising a school

5. Although your school isn't a profit-making business, it does provide a service. Using the information about business structures and organisations, produce a business structure for your school. You would obviously start with the head teacher at the top. Before you begin you may wish to work with a partner to make a list of the different roles you know that staff do in your school; for example, deputy heads, assistant heads, heads of year, department heads, etc.
6. Imagine you are going on *Dragons' Den*. In pairs, think of a product you would want to get funding for. Pitch your product to your partner, explaining the type of business structure you would employ and how you would organise it.

ACTIVITY

Structuring my own business

7. Which type of business structure would you feel most comfortable leading and why? Discuss your answer with others in the group.

The world of business

According to a study released by Vodafone (2009), one-third of the UK's working population will be in self-employed businesses by 2015. With 75 per cent of new businesses currently failing within the first three years, it is essential that anyone considering setting up their own business gives themselves the best opportunity by having a detailed business plan and understanding key economic and business terminology.

Business plan

In order to set up a business, most people will need to borrow money, usually in the form of a bank loan. In order to secure finance, they will need to convince the bank that their business has a good chance of success. To do this a detailed business plan will need to be written, which outlines the following.

a) **Give an executive summary:** Explain the reason for establishing the business and include your business goals and company name. Include whether or not ambitious growth is expected or if it will be a regular, steady trading level.

b) **Aims of the business:** Explain the aims and targets of the business and identify any features that make it different from its rivals.

c) **Product and service:** Explain in detail the products and services on offer and include information about the market you are targeting for your product. Mention rival companies and what differentiates you from them.

d) **Marketing strategy:** How will you go about selling your product? Think about who your target market is and the advertising, promotion and price strategies you will use – the 5Ps (see page 117).

e) **Management team:** Who are the key people involved in your business? Explain their different roles and the experience and expertise they will bring to your new venture.

f) **Financial forecasts:** Explain any finance that is provided by the management team, the risks and how any of the risks can be reduced. You should include details of sales forecast, future profits and losses for up to five years ahead and how much you will need to borrow. Figures should be realistic so it might be worthwhile seeking the assistance of an accountant.

g) **Appendices:** Include detailed information about product specifications, competition and CVs of the management team.

In this topic you will learn about:

- the importance of a detailed business plan
- key economic and business terminology.

You will explore:

- what is needed for a successful business plan
- definitions of economic and business terminology.

ACTIVITY

Employed or self-employed?

1. Discuss why you think more and more people in the UK are setting up their own businesses.

ACTIVITY

Business plans

2. Why are business plans so important when setting up a new business?

Key economic and business terminology

Source 1 Economic and business terms

Source 1 gives a list of some well-known economic and business terms. Some of them you will look at in more detail in other topics.

1. **Accounting** – the system for recording, reporting, and evaluating financial transactions that affect a business; it processes all aspects of a business's financial performance, from payroll and other costs to revenue from making sales
2. **Assets** – the value of everything a company owns and uses to conduct its business, e.g. money, machinery, property, land, staff, etc.
3. **Business** – an organisation whose purpose is to make money
4. **Business to Business (B2B)** – one business sells goods or services to another business
5. **Business to Consumer (B2C)** – a business sells goods or services directly to the end user
6. **Cash flow** – the amount of cash generated and used by a company in a given period
7. **Contract** – a formal agreement to do work for pay
8. **Depreciation** – the value an item reduces by over time; for example, the lorries used by a haulage company will be worth a great deal less after a few years than their original cost
9. **Entrepreneur** – someone who organises, manages and takes on the risk of starting a new business
10. **Expenses** – the costs that a business incurs through its operations, such as supplies, equipment, wages, etc.
11. **Finance** – the management of money, banking, investments and credit
12. **Fixed cost** – a one-time expense that doesn't vary with volume, e.g. the cost of buying a new storage depot
13. **Forecast** – predictions about how much money you will make or lose
14. **Gross profit** – the amount of money the business makes minus the cost of any goods and services needed to produce it, e.g. raw materials, labour, marketing, etc.
15. **Industry** – a category of like businesses, e.g. manufacturing
16. **Invoice** – a bill that is issued by the seller to the buyer informing them of how much they need to pay
17. **Liabilities** – the value of what a business owes to someone else
18. **Management** – the act of organising and running a business to accomplish goals and objectives
19. **Marketing** – the advertising and promotional methods used by a company to sell its products in order to achieve sales
20. **Net income/profit** – revenues minus expenses
21. **Net worth** – the total value of a business
22. **Opportunity cost** – money spent on one thing means that it can't be spent on something else – choices have to be made
23. **Payback period** – the amount of time it takes to recover the initial investment of a business
24. **Product** – something produced or manufactured to be sold
25. **Profit margin** – the ratio of profit divided by revenue displayed as a percentage, e.g. if a company makes £2,000,000 but £1,000,000 was spent on producing their goods, their profit margin would be 50%
26. **Return on investment (ROI)** – how much money a business gets in return from an investment, e.g. if a company makes £1,000,000 but the cost of raw materials, time spent by workers, research, marketing, etc. adds up to £750,000, then the ROI would be £250,000

27. **Revenue** – the entire amount of income before expenses are subtracted

28. **Sales prospect** – a potential customer

29. **Supplier** – an organisation that provides supplies or a service to a business

30. **SWOT analysis** – an evaluation of the **S**trengths and **W**eaknesses of a product or service and any **O**pportunities or **T**hreats associated with it, e.g. other companies that might be making the same product

31. **Target market** – a specific group of customers at which a company aims its products and services

32. **Variable cost** – expenses that change depending on the activity of a business and volume of goods, e.g. the price of petrol or diesel for a haulage company will change on a regular basis

ACTIVITY

The language of business

3. Make a copy of the table below. Put each of the economic and business terms in Source 1 into the correct category.

Organisation	Money	People	Product	Publicity

4. Is there one category that is more important than any of the others in the successful running of a business? Explain your answer.

Many of the business terms you looked at related to promoting a product to a certain market in order to make a profit. When marketing a product you need to consider the 5Ps: the right **product**, at the right **price**, to the right **people**, in the right **place**, with the right **promotion**.

ACTIVITY

Marketing a product

5. Choose a well-known company or brand and explain how it achieves the 5Ps marketing mix. An example for McDonald's can be seen in Source 2.

Source 2

McDonald's – the 5Ps

Product: Fast-food burgers, chips, etc.

Price: A range of low prices affordable by all.

People: All age ranges are targeted, but particularly children and teenagers. Families are also targeted to regard it as a treat, or as a 'quick bite to eat' whilst out.

Place: McDonald's restaurants can be found everywhere, from city centres to motorway service stations.

Promotion: A range of promotions including Monopoly games, Happy Meal film promotions, 99p saver menu, festive menus, etc.

ACTIVITY

Risk-taker or not?

6. Can you ever see yourself setting up your own business? Do you see yourself as a risk-taker or not? Explain why.

The how and why of business financing

In this topic you will learn about:

- the reasons businesses need financing
- the types of finance available to businesses
- the importance of businesses in society.

You will explore:

- internal and external finance
- the advantages and disadvantages of different types of finance
- which types of finance are most appropriate for which products.

One of the most important factors in business is profit. However, before any business can make a profit, it needs finance to start up – maybe to buy equipment or help with the day-to-day running of the company. Sometimes finance will be needed for a short period of time – maybe to overcome a shortage of funds; for example, if a customer hasn't paid on time – whilst on other occasions it may be needed for much longer; for example, if a new building or large machinery is being purchased.

Business finance

There are two main types of finance available to businesses. These are **internal** and **external** finance.

Internal finances are those that come from within the business itself. There is no cost to the business as such, but by funding one particular aspect of a business it could mean that you no longer have enough to fund something else. This is known as the **opportunity cost**. An example would be if you have used funding to purchase new premises, which could mean that you can't afford to buy new equipment.

External finances usually involve borrowing money and paying back an additional amount in the form of **interest**, or giving away a share in the business. To secure external finance a business may be asked to provide **security** in the form of an asset owned by the business; for example, property or machinery. If the business is unable to keep up payments, the asset can be sold to reclaim the money owed.

The type of external finance a business chooses is influenced by the amount it needs to borrow and what it needs it for. This, in turn, affects how long it needs the loan for and the amount of time it needs to pay it back; for example, you wouldn't choose an overdraft to pay for company cars as you would want to lease these over a longer period of time.

Source 1 shows examples of the types of external finance available.

Source 1 The finance timeline

Short term (usually up to 12 months)	Medium term (usually 1–3 years)	Long term (usually more than 3 years)
Overdraft from bank **Factoring** **Trade/store credit**	**Bank loan** **Hire purchase/ lease** **Grant**	Bank loan **Mortgage** Hire purchase/lease **Venture capital/ new investor**

ACTIVITY

Why businesses need finance

1. a) In pairs make a list of all the reasons you can think of why new businesses need finance.

b) Choose a particular type of business of interest to you and number each reason for finance in your list in order in order of importance for your choice.

c) Discuss:

- Was it difficult to number your reasons in order of importance?
- If so, what does this suggest about the difficulties businesses have when starting up or allocating finance?
- Were there any reasons that had to be financed for the business to work?

ACTIVITY

Business financing

2. In small groups choose one or two of the different types of business finance in Source 1 (look up any terms you don't understand in the glossary). Use the internet to research:
   a) how the finance is given
   b) examples of this type of finance.
   Feed back the information you have found to the class.

3. A business uses finance for a variety of reasons. Make a copy of the table below. Using the information in Source 2, decide which type of finance is most appropriate for each. Add any other examples you can think of.

Overdraft/ credit	Bank loan	Hire purchase/ lease	Mortgage	Company profits	Investor

4. Read each of the scenarios in Source 3. For each one give advice as to what type of finance is most appropriate and why. You may need to advise using more than one source of finance.

Source 2 Reasons for finance

a) Temporary shortage of funds
b) Equipment
c) Advertising
d) Company cars, lorries, etc.
e) Computers
f) Buying property/premises
g) Start-up costs
h) New premises (not owned by the business)
i) 'Buying' goods before paying for them
j) New staff
k) Staff training
l) Research and development

Source 3 Finance scenarios

a) A brand new business wishes to sell video games, DVDs and music over the internet and needs money for the appropriate computer technology, stock, etc.

b) A small independent gardening business (one person) wishes to buy a second-hand lorry and employ a new member of staff.

c) A well-established florist wants to expand their business by relocating to bigger premises on the main shopping street in their town centre. They also want to expand their product to include balloons, chocolates and other goods that can be delivered with their flowers.

ACTIVITY

The importance of business

5. Why are businesses, whatever their size, so important to our society? What problems would we have if businesses couldn't get finance when they needed it?

Entrepreneurship and risk

In this topic you will learn about:

- what it means to be enterprising
- managing risks within business
- the qualities needed to be a successful entrepreneur.

You will explore:

- successful entrepreneurs and the products that have made them successful
- SWOT analyses and how they can be used to reduce risks in business
- the role of teamwork in enterprise.

You will no doubt have heard of names such as Sir Richard Branson, Lord Alan Sugar and Bill Gates. Each of them has become very famous and also very rich. They are what are known as **entrepreneurs**. An entrepreneur is an individual who takes calculated financial risks to launch a new financial venture or business.

Source 1

Case Study: Duncan Bannatyne

This former king of the 99s made money from an ice cream van before moving on to nursing homes and health clubs.

Duncan Bannatyne was born in Glasgow on 2 February 1949. He left school at 15 with no formal qualifications and he has said that he was easily distracted in school by the thought of the money he was making from his paper round. He joined the navy and trained as a mechanic.

A poverty-stricken childhood steeled Duncan's drive to make his fortune from an early age. After his naval career, which included a spell in military prison, Duncan drifted from job to job ending up in Jersey. It was here that he made the decision to turn his life around.

He began his entrepreneurial life by trading in cars, but it was with an ice cream van purchased for £450 that he changed the course of his life. With 'Duncan's Super Ices', he set out to become the King of the 99 and eventually sold the business for £28,000, founding a nursing home business on the proceeds.

He sold his nursing home business for £46 million in 1996. During the last 10 years he has expanded into health clubs with the Bannatyne's chain to his name, and also owns bars, hotels and property. Bannatyne's is now the largest independent chain of health clubs in the UK. Duncan's latest venture is Bannatyne's Sensory Spa, a chain of luxury health and well-being spas.

Quoted on *The Sunday Times 2009 Rich List* as having wealth to the tune of £320 million, Duncan holds an OBE and was recently awarded an honorary Doctor of Science (DSc) from Glasgow Caledonian University for services to business and charity and an honorary Doctor of Business from the University of Teesside (DBA).

Over 30 charities have benefited from Duncan's involvement and he has recently launched the Bannatyne Charitable Trust to support worthwhile causes.

As a key member of the BBC's *Dragons' Den* programme from 2005 he has agreed investments in the Den that total £1,150,000 in 17 businesses. This means that he is encouraging other entrepreneurs to realise their dream, as well as attempting to make more profit for himself.

Adapted from www.bbc.co.uk/dragonsden/dragons/duncanbannatyne.shtml

ACTIVITY

What makes an entrepreneur?

1. a) Make a list of any other entrepreneurs you may have heard of. You may need to think of a product or service and then who created it; for example, the Dyson vacuum cleaner was created by Sir James Dyson.

b) Select one of the entrepreneurs from your list and use the internet to research them in greater detail. Produce a case study similar to the one about Duncan Bannatyne in Source 1. Try to find out the following details:

- when they were born and other personal details
- their first invention/idea
- how they got their idea 'up and running'
- when they made their first million
- any setbacks they had
- what they have done since.

c) In small groups, talk about what you found out about your entrepreneur.

- What do they all have in common?
- Did they all face the same problems?
- What do they tell you about being successful?

One of the qualities that all the people you have researched will have in common is that they are '**enterprising**'. You will have probably come across this word before, and maybe even taken part in enterprise days or events such as *Dragons' Den*-style competitions. But what qualities do you need to be enterprising? Source 2 below shows some of these. A simple way to remember these qualities are PIER: Persuasion, Idea, Energy, Risk.

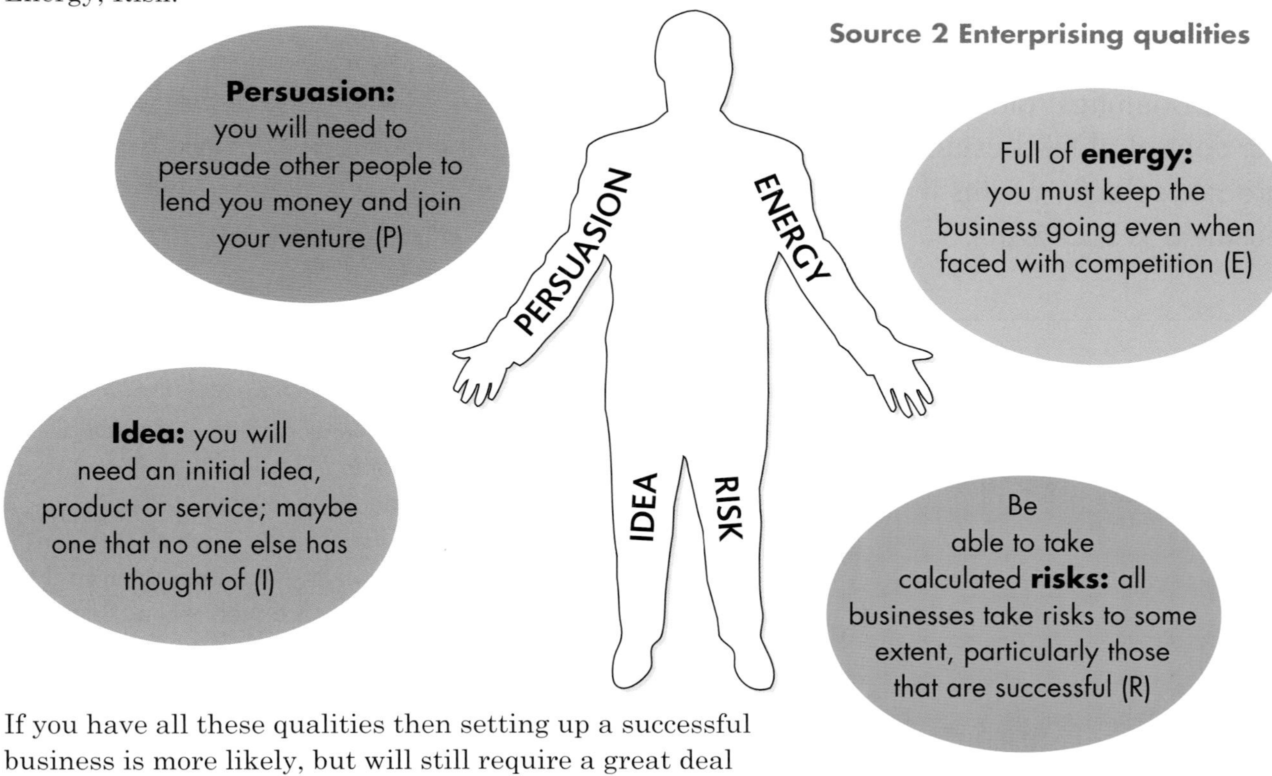

Source 2 Enterprising qualities

If you have all these qualities then setting up a successful business is more likely, but will still require a great deal of hard work and commitment. However, if you are lacking any of the qualities then success is very difficult to achieve.

Enterprise qualities

2. For each enterprise quality in Source 2 on the previous page, explain the problems an entrepreneur would face if they didn't have that quality.

3. Rank the qualities in order from the most important to the least and explain your order. Is this possible to do?

4. Why is financial risk such an important issue and a reason why many people are put off? For example, think about what could be lost if the business venture failed.

5. Do you think you have the qualities to be an entrepreneur?

6. Do you think others think you have the qualities to be an entrepreneur?

SWOT

One way to help manage risks associated with a new enterprise venture is to carry out what is called a SWOT analysis. A SWOT analysis is a strategic method that is used to evaluate the **strengths** (S), **weaknesses** (W), **opportunities** (O) and **threats** (T) of any new business ideas.

Strengths: things that the business is in control of that give it an advantage over others.	**W**eaknesses: things that the business is in control of that place the business at a disadvantage compared to others.
Opportunities: other chances outside the control of the business to make greater sales or profits if your initial business is successful.	**T**hreats: problems outside the control of the business that could put the business at risk, such as other businesses offering the same product or service.

SWOT

7. a) Read Source 3. In pairs or small groups, carry out a SWOT analysis on the Apple iPad. Use the internet to research it further if you need more specific detail.

b) Work in pairs to make a list of ways in which you can minimise the threats and maximise the opportunities for the iPad; for example, launch a webcam add-on to take pictures and use for video calling over wi-fi.

You probably identified that one of the strengths of the iPad is the 'Apple' brand name. Developing a strong brand name that customers trust is important if a business is to become a success.

Source 3

Case Study: Apple iPad

Apple is an American company that has gone from strength to strength, with much hype surrounding the new products they release. In 2010 they released the much-anticipated iPad. The tablet PC offers new technology and merges the best features of smart phones and notebook PCs. It is beautifully designed, lightweight yet strong. It has a super fast Wi-Fi connection, which means that web pages are launched extremely quickly. The high-definition display means that films and photos can be viewed as they were meant to be seen, and the battery life – lasting up to 10 hours – puts most other laptops and tablet PCs to shame. The touch screen makes using the iPad an enjoyable and very easy experience.

However, the iPad lacks a USB port, which means that information has to be transferred by Wi-Fi rather than USB memory stick. Unlike the iPhone, the iPad doesn't have a camera so can't be used for Skype and other Wi-Fi video calling. The lack of multi-tasking on the iPad gives laptop PCs the edge, as does the lack of a full-size keyboard.

In addition to the actual iPad itself, the ability to download 'apps' (as with the iPhone), offering a huge range of new tools, games and software, has seen the iPad market grow even further. Other businesses have seized the opportunity and developed their own 'apps', which can be bought from the online 'app store'. Apple will no doubt release a second version of the iPad, which is rumoured to feature both a camera and multi-tasking capabilities.

The price of the iPad will prevent many from owning one, who in turn may seek cheaper alternatives, which are now on the market for around £150. It may also be in competition with its sister products such as the MacBook and iPhone.

A world without risk

8. What would the world be like if we didn't have entrepreneurs who are prepared to be enterprising and take positive risks?

Glossary

Abilities A natural tendency to do something successfully or well. Abilities can be developed through learning and practice.
APR (annual percentage rate) Used to calculate the amount of interest you will pay each year for your loan. The higher the APR the more interest you will pay. You should always check the APR for any loan, credit card or store card. Some are about 10 per cent whereas others are 15 per cent or even 30 per cent. They usually have a decimal place, so 29.9 per cent is practically 30 per cent.
Asylum seeker A person who applies for protection and the right of residence in a foreign country.
Bank loan Money given to an individual or business, which has to be repaid over a set period of time and will include interest.
Body image The picture each of us has in our head of how we look – our appearance, our shape, our size – and how we feel and think about our bodies.
Centralised structure The head office of a business retains the major responsibilities for big decisions and powers.
Collaborative structure Collaboration takes place between a company and its partners, suppliers, investors and customers.
Credit A contractual agreement in which a borrower receives something of value now and agrees to repay the lender at some later date.
Credit cards Credit card companies loan you up to an agreed amount of money and issue you with a card to buy goods with it. You can use them in shops and also when buying online or over the phone. As they are loans, you have to pay an amount of interest depending on the APR of the card. Each month you must make a minimum payment, but if you only pay this then the debt will increase as the interest charged is usually more than the minimum. The credit card will have a limit but remember this is the limit of how much the company will lend you – you still have to pay it all back as well as the interest. You should only use credit if you know you have, or will have, the money to make the repayments.
Credit crunch The reduction in the amount of disposable income people have and in the general availability of bank loans, etc.
Cult of celebrity The widespread interest in famous individuals. This has become the main focus of many popular "reality" television programmes.
Debt Money that is owed or due to someone else. This includes loans, mortgages, credit card payments or money you owe to another individual.
Default on a mortgage When a person stops making the repayments on the loan they have taken to pay for their flat/house without informing the lender.
Deficit model In this book 'deficit model' is used to describe the technique that suggests we can always do more to make ourselves more acceptable.
Developing country Generally used to describe a nation with a low level of material well-being. Since no single definition of the term is recognised internationally, the levels of development may vary widely within so-called developing countries.
Discrimination A prejudiced attitude affecting the way an individual or group is treated, usually less favourably.
Disposable income The amount of money that is left to spend or save once all bills such as the mortgage and credit cards have been paid.
Drug economy In this book, it refers to the huge amounts of money that change hands and the numbers of people who earn their living from trading in illegal drugs.
Emotional health The part of our overall health that is concerned with the way we think and feel. It refers to our sense of well-being and our ability to cope with life events. Emotional health is about our ability to acknowledge and respect our own emotions as well as those of others.
Employed Someone who is in paid work; they are employed.
Entrepreneur A person who has a new idea, product or venture and leads in its development.
Ethical consumerism Adopting an ethical perspective on our disposable income. It involves the intentional purchase of products and services that the customer considers to be made ethically. This may mean with minimal harm to or exploitation of humans, animals and/or the natural environment.
External finance A business seeks money from outside the company rather than using their own profits.
Factoring A company sells their invoices at a discounted rate to a third company for immediate payment. The third company can then 'chase' money from invoiced companies.
Globalisation The process by which regional economies, societies and cultures have become integrated through a global network of political ideas through communication, transportation and trade.
Grant Money given by one group (e.g. government) to another, for a specific reason (often non-profit). This has to be applied for.
Hire purchase/lease A monthly fee is paid to hire or lease equipment, e.g. company car.
Illegal drugs Drugs that a person is not allowed to have, e.g. cannabis, cocaine, heroin, etc. If a person is caught with illegal drugs, they may be punished. Drugs that are considered illegal vary from country to country.
Interest The fee paid to borrow money.
Internal finance A business uses its own profits to finance new projects rather than borrowing or seeking other investment.
Legal drugs Drugs that a person may use within the law, e.g. alcohol, tobacco, prescribed medicines.
LGB Lesbian, gay or bisexual.
Matrix structure A business structure created by teams of people from various sections of a business. Often used for a specific project.
Money/debt adviser A person specifically trained to offer advice both on debt and on increasing your income. A money or debt adviser can help you work out what your options are and, where needed, negotiate affordable payments and set up repayment plans with your creditors. They work in the private, public and voluntary sectors, so you may get advice from a money or debt adviser in a private company that specialises in dealing with debt, or through your council or a voluntary organisation or charity such as the Citizens Advice Bureau or a credit union.

Mortgage A loan taken out to buy a property.
Negative risk The undesired outcome of doing something that damages well-being, e.g. dependency on drugs and alcohol, carrying a weapon, exceeding the speed limit.
Newly industrialised country In the 20th century many countries in east and south east Asia were developing their economies. These nations are called newly industrialised countries or NICs. They are also sometimes referred to as tiger economies because of their rapid growth rate.
NGO Non-governmental organisation – a legally constituted organisation that operates independently of any government.
Niche product A product that is designed to satisfy a specific, maybe unusual, demand in the market.
Nuclear family Historically this has been seen as a household consisting of two married, heterosexual parents and their legal children.
Opportunity cost The financial impact of choosing one thing over another. Money spent on one product means it is not available to spend on anything else.
Overdraft An agreed amount by which your bank account can be overdrawn – an amount more than you have in your account. If you have an overdraft facility of £200 you can spend up to £200 more than is in your account. Generally you will be charged a set fee for the overdraft and interest on the amount you are overdrawn. If you go over the agreed amount of your overdraft you will be subject to additional fees or charges.
Personal support network A group of people that can consist of friends, family members, relatives, professionals, co-workers and neighbours who you can use to seek support from.
Positive risk The intended outcome of doing something that is beneficial to well-being, e.g. sports, performing on stage, speaking in public, going for a job interview.
Prejudice An attitude that pre-judges how someone may think or feel about something or someone else, often not based on experience or fact. This is usually a negative outlook.
Profit The amount of money a business or individual makes after paying for materials, employees and other costs.
Qualities The essential or distinctive characteristics or attributes of a person; a personality or character trait, e.g. 'kindness is one of her many good qualities'.
Redundancy Occurs when the company you work for can no longer afford to employ you as they do not have enough business coming in. 'Redundant' literally means 'not needed'.
Refugee An exile who flees from their own country for safety. This may be as a result of war, natural disaster or being persecuted for reasons such as their race, religion, nationality, membership of a particular social group or political opinion.
Repossession If you buy your house with the help of a loan then the lender will usually protect their interest by registering a 'legal charge' against your house. This means that when the house is sold you will first have to repay the lender any money you have outstanding. If you do not keep up the repayments on the loan the lender can repossess your property. This means they can take over the property and sell it in order to pay back the loan.
Rights and responsibilities Balancing the things to which we feel entitled (our rights) with the obligations (our responsibilities) we have to other people and society.
Secured consolidation loan A loan where you are required to use your property as security against the loan, so the lender is able to balance the risk of lending to you. If you default on the loan your home is at risk of being taken from you to pay the debt.
Security Financial security is having a greater income than expenditure and saving on a regular basis. This may take the form of money in the bank or investment in property. Security means that you have something of financial worth that is likely to increase in value over time.
Self-employed Working for yourself rather than another person or organisation.
Sexually healthy A sexually healthy person understands that sex can have various outcomes, ranging from pleasure to conception to transmission of STIs, and behaves responsibly.
Social marketing Using advertisements and marketing messages to influence behaviours, not to benefit the advertiser, but to benefit the person being targeted by the campaign and society in general.
Social networking An online service, platform or site that focuses on building relationships among people, e.g. those who share interests and/or activities.
Stereotype A common belief held about groups of people within society, which can be reinforced through the media.
STI Sexually transmitted infection.
Store cards Issued by a particular shop for buying goods from them on credit. They are a useful way of paying for goods if you shop a lot at the same store. However, a lot of people use them when they do not have enough money to pay for the goods. As they are loans, you have to pay interest and some of these cards have a high APR, which means you can pay back a lot more than the goods cost, especially if you need a long time to pay. The more store cards you have, the more of a problem this can be. You should only use store cards when you know you will be able to afford to pay the money back.
Stress The feeling of being under pressure. Too much pressure or prolonged pressure can lead to stress, which is unhealthy for the mind and body.
Student loan Organised by the government, repayment only starts when you are earning over a certain sum of money. The amount loaned will depend on your family income and circumstances. These loans are for the full year and should cover living costs during holidays as well as term time.
Trade union An organisation made up mainly of workers who pay a membership subscription. Trade unions try to form good relationships with employers and negotiate on their members' behalf.
Trade/store credit Credit given by a store so you can buy goods and pay later.
Venture capital/new investor Money that is provided in the early stages of high-potential new projects to fund start-up costs or expand a business. A stake in the company is given in return.
Voluntary work Being motivated to work without the need of financial reward. Often linked to a cause of interest to an individual.

Index